Practice

Practice

Unleashing the Power of Faith

by Jane Jayroe

OKLAHOMA HALL of FAME
PUBLISHING

Printed in Canada

ISBN: 978-1-938923-40-1
LIBRARY OF CONGRESS CONTROL NUMBER: 2018960285

Cover Photo: Sunrise from Emerald Vista on Winding Stair Mountain, Ouachita National Forest along the Talimena Scenic Drive in southeastern Oklahoma by David Fitzgerald.

Back Cover Photo: Charlie Neuenschwander.

Cover and Interior Design: Skip McKinstry

DEDICATION

To my husband Jerry, whose support moves my
seemingly out-of-reach ideas into rewarding realities.

TABLE OF CONTENTS

FOREWORD

PRACTICE: UNLEASHING THE POWER OF FAITH.
What will we choose to practice today, God's presence or the presence of problems? Every day we practice something — busyness, anger, envy, depression, anxiety, love, peace, and/or joy. Today's habits become our future. Outside demands can push us around every minute. To play our best, at the game of life's circumstances, let's plug into the power of faith. We do that by practicing our devotion to God.

Growing spiritually strong doesn't begin with a set of dumbbells, a Wall Street update, or merely the repetition of affirmations. Having a *daily time with God* nurtures us—a tiny seed of availability—into a towering tree of faith.

We can't always control what happens. We can, however, boost the mind and heart to a higher level of spiritual strength with holy habits. Focusing on inspiration that sets our minds on God and good, matters.

What follows in this book are not happily-ever-after fairy tales, but reminders of our own deep identity as children of God. We are not our jobs, our family, our political affiliations, our bank statements—we are believers trying to mature into the people God has created us to be.

The men and women you'll soon meet found the strength to hold on when things fell apart. They learned lessons from life's messes or simply showed us how to live *on purpose and in love.*

So whether you're facing a mountain of problems or simply need encouragement, begin now a routine of finding God in the nooks and crannies, in the doubts and dreams of your life.

About a decade ago I made the decision to spend time with God every morning. I began by asking God to help me wake up earlier in order to fit this extra commitment into my schedule. To my amazement, my eyes opened before the alarm sounded and, for five years, I never missed a day. Then, I let it slip. I continued to pray and read and worship. But I let the details of life overtake my priorities …on first one day, then two, and before long I had gone a week with "devotional" on my calendar, but never marked off.

I missed the growth, the closeness. I needed help to get back on track.

A small group of Christian friends who wanted this same kind of encouragement and accountability agreed to meet weekly. Joining with others, either in person or online, is a great help. Several times, I have benefited from studying the St. Ignatius Exercises in a group setting.

When I begin my day with God, and centered in scripture, I am growing and unleashing the power of faith. When I read about lessons of courage and trust in the lives of others, I am blessed. May you be as well.

How to use the book:

Practice: Unleashing the Power of Faith, shares a story a day. To maximize the impact of a dedicated sacred time, find a designated space for your reading, reflection, and praying—a specific chair, an appointed time. Distance yourself from outside distractions. Susannah Wesley, mother of nineteen children including Wesley and Charles, who founded the Methodist movement, simply sat with her apron over her head. It was a sign to the family that she was talking to God and was not to be disturbed.

Get comfortable. I'm delighted to have a chair near a window where I can witness God's canvas of nature and breathe in the changing seasons.

After reading the daily story, enter into a time of silence. Just be with God. If outside thoughts rush in, let them come, then let them go. If something in the story or in the scripture "shimmers" or rises to the top of your mind, let it bloom. Be open to God speaking to you in that place.

Listen for God's whispers.

After this silent time, journal your thoughts. What insight did you gain through your quiet time—the story—the scripture? If you stay with the discipline, insight will come but by grace, not by effort.

Throughout the day, practice what God teaches you from the story. At night, before you sleep, thank God. Reflect on the day, with appreciation and awareness of where God showed up in your day.

Finally, consider using this book in a small group. It will multiply your daily encounters with God and promote conversation and friendship within your circle. A discussion guide has been created and is available online at janejayroe.com

Daily time with God improves relationships, decisions, and attitudes. Instead of living with hurry and worry, choose trust and thanksgiving instead.

JANE JAYROE

PRACTICE THINKING

IN CERTAIN WAYS
—TRUSTING ME,
THANKING ME—
AND THOSE THOUGHTS
BECOME MORE NATURAL.

SARA YOUNG

Jesus Calling

...FOR THE JOY OF THE LORD IS YOUR STRENGTH.

NEHEMIAH 8:10

In high school, I was a fish out of water. At 4'11", with a high speaking voice and a passion for the arts, I was a target for teasing. One day someone wanted to beat me up after school and I told her, "Look, it's not even worth the punch." She just walked away. My instinct has often been to put people at ease and to have fun.

My cheerful personality hasn't always been an asset. Sometimes people think, *she's a fake.* Truth is, I *am* a happy person. I kinda' get tired of apologizing for that. My joy is not because my life is easy or perfect, but because my faith is strong and I work to keep a positive outlook. I've had hard times, but I decided years ago that I could stay stuck and be bitter or I could continue on and be happy. God has given me amazing opportunities, the most supportive family possible, and musical gifts. I'm grateful …and happy.

My singing career began in church, at the age of seven, and Christian music will always have a place in my heart. Recently, for my "Coming Home" concert in my hometown of Broken Arrow, I sang "Upon This Rock." With the young voices from the high school choir behind me, and my friends and family sitting in front of me, it was as though God's blessings of my whole history was just pouring through my body.

While growing up in that Oklahoma suburban community, I always dreamed of performing. I didn't realize some of the sacrifices involved—like not having the kind of family life that I had benefitted from, of grueling travel schedules, and a number of health battles. It's a daily challenge to find the time to listen to God, to hear His voice in this loud demanding world.

From that Oklahoma high school, I was blessed to find the right road for my career at Oklahoma City University where I earned my Bachelor's and Masters degrees. Then it was the role on Broadway in *You're a Good Man, Charlie Brown* that earned me a Tony Award and started a career that I could never have imagined.

Whether revealing the heart of a character I portray in a movie, in a television series, on a stage, or singing lyrics that touch people's hearts, or showing love to the people around me—I want to make an impact for good. I am not the type of person who stands on a street corner and shouts, "I'm a Christian!" What happens, really by accident, is that people I'm working with say, "Why are you so happy?"

God works in my life. If you could hang around me for one week, you would only begin to see the miracles that happen.

The first miraculous event was my family. I'm adopted and God set up the most amazing parents and brother for me. My parents' love has supported my life and career in remarkable ways. They gave me such a strong sense of security. Even though they weren't performers, they felt that God had given me this vocal gift and they helped me develop it. To this day, their constant prayers mean the world to me.

I'm a big believer in prayer. I pray walking down the street in New York. I pray on the plane. I pray without shutting my eyes. I pray for my family and friends. I pray for complete strangers. But just because I'm frank about my faith doesn't mean I've got it all figured out. I struggle, too. It's like developing your vocal range when you're a singer. You've got to experience the highs and lows to develop a spiritual range and grow in your faith.

Does my faith mean that bad things don't happen? Like falling off a stage? Or getting a Meniere's disease attack which makes the world spin so badly I can't walk across the room? No. Tough things happen, that's life. But my joy is deeper than those circumstances and His presence allows me to keep coming back.

Yes, I get depressed. I gripe. I fall into a perfectionist's funk. And yet, I'm thankful every day. For my family, my friends, my career, my voice, even for setbacks and struggles. When I laugh, when I sing, when I love, when I live in His light…joy abounds.

KRISTIN CHENOWETH

Professional Singer/Actress, Author, Oklahoma Hall of Fame Inductee
Broken Arrow, OK

ABBA, FATHER HE SAID, "EVERYTHING IS POSSIBLE FOR YOU.
TAKE THIS CUP FROM ME. YET NOT WHAT I WILL,
BUT WHAT YOU WILL."

MARK 14:36

We are raised by our communities—family, parishioners, teachers, leaders, peers. Community helps us understand our role as part of something larger than ourselves. Faith has always shaped and influenced my communities. Faith has formed my character and set the standards and morals that guide my life.

My father, a full-blood Chickasaw, passed away unexpectedly in the late 1940s, when I was two years old. My mother was left with six children—age two to 14—to raise and provide for. A woman of high standards and strong faith, my mother lived her life in a manner that provided a great foundation and example for us.

Growing up, I was a member of a Baptist church and part of a church family. My entire church family joined in the celebration when I was baptized at the age of 12 in my hometown of Tishomingo.

Faith is strong in a small community, and Tishomingo has always epitomized the best of what it means to be a small community. My teachers, Boy Scout leaders, and the adults in my life all were faithful people. Their faith translated to the classroom, the campsite, and to everyday life. It wasn't what they said, but how they lived their life that made them such impactful role models.

My experience as a Boy Scout has had a great influence on my life. Duty to God and country form the foundation of the oath. Being trustworthy, loyal, kind, and helpful were among the expectations that came with being a Scout. Perhaps even more important is the expectation of reverence for God. For me, reverence is a mix of respect and the sense of awe that comes when we contemplate God's love and power. These expectations remain as relevant today as they were the day I took the oath.

Faith and spirituality have been engrained in the Chickasaw people since time immemorial. A sense of spirituality that comes with believing in a higher power has always played a role in who we are. Chickasaws became connected with Christian denominations before moving to Indian Territory. While faith has always played a role in our government, our government does not dictate faith.

Our practices today are a continuum of how we lived centuries ago. We recognize Indian churches of all denominations and we are always available to help. Through our legislature, we help ensure that churches of all denominations have the support they need. There is a balance of faith and spirituality embedded in all we do.

From my parents and teachers in the classroom to Scout leaders and leadership in the Chickasaw Nation, I always have been blessed with strong leaders. I have learned that those of faith tend to set higher standards for themselves as well as those around them. I have learned that, with faith, all is possible, all is bearable, and all is worth being thankful for.

GOVERNOR BILL ANOATUBBY

Governor of The Chickasaw Nation
Tishomingo/Ada, OK

FOR IT IS BY GRACE YOU HAVE BEEN SAVED, THROUGH FAITH –
AND THIS IS NOT FROM YOURSELVES, IT IS THE GIFT OF GOD –
NOT BY WORKS, SO THAT NO ONE CAN BOAST.

EPHESIANS 2:8-9

Jo Bob had it all. He was tall and trim, handsome, with dimples that flashed when he smiled his gap-toothed grin. He was witty, smart, and lucky. Lucky like the person who always got his name drawn in a raffle. He was successful in business, had a million friends, and could quickly diffuse a difficult situation with his easy "aw shucks" kind of humor and good-naturedness. He loved almost all kinds of athletics and was pretty good at many of them. He filled up a room. And, I am lucky, too, because he was my husband.

It was hard to believe that he would be a victim of younger onset Alzheimer's Disease at the age of 56. How was it possible that someone so vibrant, so full of life, would become a total dependent unable to put his own socks on, eat with a fork, walk much of a distance, or converse. He could do nothing to entertain himself. He couldn't read the paper, follow a story or a sporting event on television, or figure out what club to use in golf or where to aim the ball. It was heartbreaking to see that he had to give up his beloved fishing because he became afraid to step in the boat and unable to figure out what to do with a pole. As his capabilities began to diminish, his anxieties skyrocketed. It was like watching an onion be peeled—layer by layer—the parts of his personality that made him Jo Bob were rolled back and thrown away.

For me, these were desperate times. The man I had loved for almost forty years was slipping away, piece by piece, like the fade-out at the end of a movie, and there was nothing I could do that would change that. I went to support groups, took him to adult day care groups so that I could have a break

6

from care giving, and I depended on family and friends to help me carry the burden. I think I would have gone insane without the help of Jo Bob's sister Jana and her husband Dave, our daughters Leslie, Sheila, and Maggie who lived close, and other dear friends like Bob and Ruthie who would meet us for dinner at 4:00 on Tuesdays when I would pick him up from day care. Really, who goes to dinner at 4:00?

Here is what I learned. Actually I already knew this, but only in my head. Alzheimer's showed me how to have it in my heart. I learned that sometimes there is nothing to be done except endure what has been given, and I learned that prayer and relying on my Lord when I was desperate and exhausted could give me the grace I needed to go another hour. Or two. Or even a day.

Peace I give you. My peace I leave with you.

These words from the gospel of John were my bulwark through years of Jo Bob's increasing disability, but there was yet another and different hurtle to overcome that would require a different gift. This was the gift of forgiveness of myself. It was hard to forgive myself for being cross or short or for any kind of unloving behavior as I struggled to define what my new role as a wife was to be. Eventually when I decided I could no longer physically take care of him and placed him in a residential facility, I had to learn to forgive myself for not going it alone. It has been a bit of a road, this self-forgiveness thing, but God, I find, does not expect us to manage life perfectly. He just expects us to ask Him to stand with us in the midst of whatever might come, trusting in His love, patiently waiting for the grace to live each day.

But take heart. I have overcome the world!

MARY ANN HILLE

Co-Founder, Hille Foundation
Tulsa, OK

WHATEVER YOUR HAND FINDS TO DO, DO IT WITH ALL YOUR MIGHT.

ECCLESIASTES 9:10

In my mind's eye, I can still see her hands scraping out the final bits of batter from a bowl, sewing a seam in one of the dresses she'd made for herself, opening her Bible to prepare for a class she would teach. My mother may have been insignificant by worldly standards—no wealth, power, or wide spread influence—but she shaped the lives of her six children and advanced the Kingdom of God in amazing ways.

Marie Green married a preacher, the man who would become my dad. They never led a church with more than 50 members or earned more than $138 a week. Yet she taught us about generosity.

Five of her six children entered into some kind of full-time Christian service. I was considered something of a black sheep in the family because I went into business. In time, we all realized that this could be a form of ministry as well. When I received my first promotion to manager of the retail store where I worked, Mom said, "That's wonderful, David. And what are you doing for the Lord?"

I could have come home and told her I had been elected President of the United States and she would have asked the same question: "What are you doing for the Lord?"

Growing up, most of our homes were small parsonages provided by the churches we served. Often they had two bedrooms so at least two kids slept on a rollaway bed somewhere. Mom never complained. She could stretch food, patch clothes, and still manage to give to others. Never did missionaries speak to our church without Mom placing something in the offering plate for them. Our parents put about as much into their churches as they received. As I look back, I'm not sure how we made it but we were happy and healthy…not a broken bone or an illness among us.

Mom lived generosity and integrity, every day. I had to learn what that meant in the business world. When Hobby Lobby began to grow and become a multi-state business, a new competitor in the craft market business moved in with stores open seven days a week. Our stores had always been closed on Sundays so employees could go to church. Further, the new competitor boasted $100-million in stock sales and a plan to bury Hobby Lobby. We got scared. All our humanness showed up and we felt that, if they were open on Sundays, we would have to be as well. It appeared to be the right business decision. Over the next several years, Hobby Lobby began averaging about $100-million in business on Sundays alone.

But I knew in my heart that this wasn't the right spiritual decision. In time, we decided to be faithful to God's calling and close on Sundays even though I was anxious about taking the hit of that loss. We decided to scale back the closings and see how it went …first we would close the three Nebraska stores. A newspaper picked up the story and when I read that headline, it felt like such a poor witness. It was as if I was saying that I was willing to be obedient to God *only if it paid dividends*. We quickly decided to close *all* the stores on Sundays because we believed God wanted us to honor Him in this way.

For the next two years, profits dropped. We stayed the course, and profits came back—stronger than ever. I really feel that you either believe God's Word, or you don't. I believe. And I want to walk in obedience to it.

That same integrity caused my family to wind up in the U.S. Supreme Court in a very difficult legal fight over religious freedom. It wasn't something we wanted to do but, as owners of Hobby Lobby, we couldn't, in good faith, pay for some birth control drugs that we believed "induced" abortion. That's what the new health-care law required. It was against what we believed as Christians. The legal advice we had going in wasn't hopeful, but we never faltered. On June 30, 2014, the High Court ruled 5-4 in favor of our family business, allowing us to honor God by operating our company in a manner consistent with Biblical principles.

My mother has been gone for some time now. Her picture hangs in the lobby of our corporate office. Her values and prayers have influenced our lives so much and the lives of her grandchildren. Some days I can hardly believe what God has done with my life. From those parsonages in southwestern Oklahoma to opening our first business with a $600 loan to the joy of my family and more than 800 Hobby Lobby stores employing approximately 32,000 of the finest employees, I have been so blessed. But always I will hear my mom's voice, "what are you doing for the Lord, David?" That shapes everything.

DAVID GREEN

Founder & CEO, Hobby Lobby Stores, Inc.
Altus/Oklahoma City, OK

YEA, THOUGH I WALK THROUGH THE VALLEY OF THE SHADOW OF
DEATH, I WILL FEAR NO EVIL FOR THOU ART WITH ME.

PSALM 23:4

"Who loves ya, mama?" his laughing voice lit up my phone. Oh, my angel! Every morning at 8:30 on the dot, my grown up boy called and made my day.

Then, he was gone. And the phone at 8:30 in the morning yelled its silence as my sorrow covered everything.

My 43-year-old son, Steve, had died much too soon.

He left me the gift of precious memories …God's presence and His church.

I grew up in the church; my family was there seven days a week. The early years were good. Two preachers in our neighborhood would come pray for our family because they knew we were doing something wrong; we were having too much fun. My dad was everything in the church, but I grew tired of going.

Then, my folks got a divorce. My sweet mama was left with three of us to raise. She kept taking us to church in spite of the fact that Daddy was still there …a big deal in the church. She was just a hard working woman—doing right by her family. I didn't think the church should have kept acting like my dad was such a good guy. Another mark against the church in my eyes. I decided that when I left home, I was done with church.

When I walked down the street and saw some of those folks who I knew were going to talk about what the Lord had been doing in their life, I just turned the other way. I didn't want anything to do with them.

Now, I'm one of those folks. If you see me coming, just know that I'm going to tell you about the Lord. He saved me through the sorrow of losing Steve. I thought I was going to die from the pain of losing my child but God was with me. He comforted me. And He gave me a purpose again in public service for my community.

Before the tragedy of Steve's passing, our lives were full and happy when my son started asking me about returning to the church. I was serving as the first African American on the City Council. My boys were excelling in school. But Steve knew we needed God and needed the church even if it made mistakes at times.

Not a day goes by that I don't miss that boy. "Who loves you, mama?" still resonates in my heart, but I know my son's love is with me forever and my heavenly Father's is as well. It's enough to keep me living and loving for this lifetime.

WILLA JOHNSON

Oklahoma City Councilwoman and Oklahoma County Commissioner
Oklahoma City, OK

LOVE MUST BE SINCERE. HATE WHAT IS EVIL; CLING TO WHAT IS GOOD. BE DEVOTED TO ONE ANOTHER IN BROTHERLY LOVE.

ROMANS 12:9

On the morning following the bombing of the Alfred P. Murrah Federal Building in Oklahoma City on April 19, 1995, my wife Cathy and I went to the site to see what had occurred during the night and to determine what we, as Governor and First Lady of Oklahoma, could do to help. I knew that the first responders and rescue workers were skilled and focused professionals and needed no instruction from us. They would rescue and recover with skill and compassion. As a former FBI agent, and former supervisor of much of the federal law enforcement establishment, I knew that the investigators of this criminal horror would perform extraordinarily well without guidance from us.

When we got there, massive lights bathed the fractured building against the still black sky. The weather was chilly and a light rain fell. I noticed the figure of a firefighter walking up the street and toward us, his protective jacket slung over his shoulder. When he reached us, I could tell that he was not an Oklahoma City firefighter. He must be one of the FEMA Urban Search and Rescue workers whom President Bill Clinton promised the day before to come and to help Oklahoma City find our injured and recover our dead.

"Thank you for coming," I said as I stepped into the street to shake his hand.

"Who are you?" he asked.

"I am the governor of the state," I responded.

Unimpressed, he jabbed his finger into my chest and declared, "Then you find out who did this because all I've pulled from that rubble was a child's finger and an American flag."

He walked on up the street and into the night.

It was a shocking introduction to what we would see in the days and weeks to come. Instantly, I knew that the man was in shock: stunned, anguished, and in disbelief. How could evil of this magnitude occur? Who did this? *How could anyone do this?*

Cathy's and my duty would be to embrace and to thank and to comfort all those who came. Meals. Water. Equipment. Shoes. Clothing. Massages. In the early cell phone era, free phone calls. All would be provided as a thank you and a charge: please help us. We need you. We are grateful to you.

One day, a firefighter grabbed my arm and said with a smile that the only thing missing from his bunk when he returned at night were mints on his pillow and a rose. The next evening, Cathy saw to it that each rescue worker had mints on their pillow and a rose.

Giving and *sharing* and *caring* were our watchwords. Love and tenderness and a Christian commitment to others were the expected common denominators of all.

Out of evil, good can come. Out of heartbreak and disbelief, faith and focus can arise.

Oklahoma City came together. We showed our neighbors that love and brotherhood are not only aspirations, but essentials of a good and caring people.

It was a life history for the Nation.

FRANK KEATING

Former Governor of Oklahoma, President & CEO American Banking Association,
and Oklahoma Hall of Fame Inductee
Tulsa/Oklahoma City, OK

BEGIN.

FIX SOME PART OF EVERY DAY FOR PRIVATE EXERCISES. YOU MAY ACQUIRE THE TASTE, WHICH YOU HAVE NOT: WHAT IS TEDIOUS AT FIRST WILL AFTERWARD BE PLEASANT. WHETHER YOU LIKE IT OR NOT, READ AND PRAY DAILY. IT IS FOR YOUR LIFE; THERE IS NO OTHER WAY: ELSE YOU WILL BE A TRIFLER ALL YOUR DAYS.

JOHN WESLEY

BE COMPLETELY HUMBLE AND GENTLE; BE PATIENT, BEARING WITH ONE ANOTHER IN LOVE.

EPHESIANS 4:2

This is a great American story of opportunity, hard work, and incredible blessings. In 1964, Tom and Judy Love leased a gas station in Watonga, Oklahoma for $5,000. That was the beginning of Love's Travel Stops & Country Stores. In 2018, Love's has 450 Travel Stops and related businesses in 41 states with over 21,000 employees.

Philanthropists for many worthwhile causes, Tom and Judy have received almost every notable award given in our state, including induction to the Oklahoma Hall of Fame. Their hearts to help others have changed our community and beyond. They have received the highest honor given to laypeople in the Catholic Church.

In 2018, Judy continues to be a daily leader and fundraiser for community causes. Tom gets up every day to run one of America's great companies. However, when I invited him to write something for this book, his professional success isn't mentioned. As much as he loves the company and its employees, he wrote about what matters the *very* most to him: faith and family.

Tom Love, one of the greatest entrepreneurs in our country, wrote this when I emailed him about his faith life growing up in Oklahoma:

> *To be asked to submit a meaningful message for your Devotional Book has me back on my heels and frankly way out of my pay grade. But let me give you a brief overview.*
>
> *I'm number 3 in a Roman Catholic family of 7—4 boys and 3 girls. All of us went to Rosary grade school—baptized and worshiped at St. Francis Catholic Church. Our faith was relatively strictly observed on*

16

a daily basis. Three of the boys went to a pretty rigid boarding high school run by the Benedictine order of monks.

My wife, Judy, had a very similar background. We married when I got out of the military, had 4 kids, and proceeded to raise them in a traditional Catholic way.

Life's been good to us and our faith is part of our daily lives. We've been lucky to be able to practice our Catholicism and Christian belief every day. We now have 9 grandchildren who seem to be on the right track—we're proud of each of them.

Well Jane Anne, that's about as good as I can do—hope it makes the cut.

—T.

Tom Love offers down-to-earth inspiration and optimism in every part of his life. He doesn't consider himself humble because he doesn't dwell on "self" enough to notice. Tom is the most disciplined person I know and that includes how he practices his faith and loves his family. Regardless of the demands of a growing business, he was never too busy to find time for his children and now his grandchildren, attending almost all of their activities. He loves people and knows their names whether it's Love employees, a waitress, or the staff at a Thunder basketball game. He's the friendliest person in the room, always, and the most generous.

Love of God and love of people will be Tom's legacy just as surely as the big red heart on the side of highways throughout America.

Jane Jayroe with
TOM LOVE

Owner, Founder, Executive Chairman, Love's Travel Stops & Country Stores
and Oklahoma Hall of Fame Inductee
Oklahoma City, OK

I WILL SAY TO THE LORD,
"HE IS MY REFUGE AND MY FORTRESS, MY GOD, IN WHOM I TRUST."

PSALM 91:2

Harold T. "H" Holden has always been a strong and taciturn man, typical of a cowboy. A horseman and outdoorsman, he is a man who loves Oklahoma and the West. As a painter and sculptor for over fifty years, H is a man of few words but great talent, in a career that is primarily a solitary endeavor. His original paintings and twenty-two monuments grace museums, airports, universities, parks, and private collections throughout the United States and he has achieved many honors throughout his long career.

Life changed in 2007 with a diagnosis of Idiopathic Pulmonary Fibrosis, a fatal lung disease, with few treatments and no cure, absent a lung transplant. As H's health deteriorated over the next three years, his ability to do even the simplest things became impossible. He closed his studio and tried to focus on simply staying alive. Spiritual, financial, and emotional help came from our church, family, friends, and fellow artists. It was a difficult time, particularly for an independent and self-sufficient man, to become dependent for every need. H prepared himself for what appeared to be the inevitable. He talked to fellow artists about finishing up his monuments "Thank You Lord", which he was working on for our church in Enid, and "Bass Reeves", which he was completing for Ft. Smith, Arkansas. Our Pastor, Wade Burleson, and several men from Emmanuel came to the house regularly to pray with H, as our friend and H's pulmonologist Dr. Brian Whitson ministered to H's medical needs.

In 2010, we made two trips to the Nazih Zuhdi Transplant Institute in Oklahoma City as the "backup" patient, H wasn't selected for transplantation and someone else received the lung he so desperately needed. H made the decision to not return to the hospital again as a "backup". Emotionally spent, we continued to pray for a miracle and for H to be healed. I still held onto my belief that God can heal us until our last breath and beyond, but I also understood that our will is not always God's will. To all of us, it appeared that there was no way H could recover or be strong enough to even withstand surgery.

On July 2, 2010, I was looking out our kitchen window praying for God to please help us; H wasn't going to live much longer. Two minutes later our transplant coordinator Marc Miller called and told us to come to Integris, there was a donor lung for H. At this point H weighed only 135 pounds and it took an hour just to get him into the car for the trip to Oklahoma City as he was so frail, but H was at peace with whatever the outcome was going to be that day. Our daughter Shannon and I said goodbye to H as they took him to surgery, not knowing if we would see him again this side of Heaven.

We sat in the waiting room, joined by friends, as we received hourly calls about the progress of the surgery. Six hours later, H had a new lung and a new life, one not tethered to an oxygen tank.

Now seven-plus years later, it is still a miracle every day. H is painting and sculpting again, enjoying family and friends and appreciating the gift he has been given. Looking back, I recognize God's timing was perfect and He was and is with us, every small and large step of the way.

God is not done with H Holden yet and for that we are all grateful.

EDNA MAE HOLDEN
Wife of HAROLD T. "H" HOLDEN

Artist and Oklahoma Hall of Fame Inductee
Kremlin/Enid, OK

LOVE IS PATIENT, LOVE IS KIND.

1 CORINTHIANS 13:4

The biggest lesson I've learned in life is the importance of kindness. Maybe I know that so well because my early life had so little. Yet, God always put good people in my path that ultimately led to more success than I could have imagined.

Around the age of 12, I was asked to leave my mother's home with her new husband. It wasn't a happy home, but it was all I had. My dad picked me up, only to let me out a few blocks later. I didn't have a dime to my name.

Life wasn't easy. I found a room and work. I always went to school.

I would pray to God every day because I knew I needed help. I managed to survive …finding food to eat even though I refused the free lunch at school because I was too proud to accept it.

Teachers were always looking out for me. I remember my high school vice principal asking me what I wanted to be? I thought for a moment and answered, "a barber." He nodded, but then told me about a print class they were starting. Isn't that God's way? To plant that interest in me way back in high school.

I grew up in a segregated world—my church, school, college, and community. But things were changing. At Douglass High School, in Oklahoma City, I loved football and played in the first integrated game in the state—Douglass vs. Capitol Hill in 1955. I was the first black All-Stater in Oklahoma. Athletics paved the way for college, although no state school was interested in an African American quarterback.

I attended Maryland State College. After graduation, I came home and worked for *The Black Dispatch* Newspaper where I soon became a partner in the ownership. Throughout my business career, I have enjoyed a great relationship with a variety of bankers in Oklahoma City. They took a risk with me, but I took great risks too. In the early days of my career, with the support of my wife, I put up everything we had and worked night and day to create success. When we met challenges, I kept my focus and didn't let anger and bitterness ruin my dreams. We always stayed the course, even when we met strong resistance within our own community. My friends then are my friends now.

We started *The Black Chronicle* in 1979, a statewide newspaper based out of Oklahoma City that focuses on the African American community in Oklahoma. We purchased our first radio station in 1993. Today we own 25 stations in several states and have purchased the tallest radio and television tower in Oklahoma.

Our company is the largest privately-owned communications company in the state and the largest black-owned independent broadcasting company in the Nation. Our company includes real estate and controlling interest in a bank. Every day is a challenging work day.

Seems that God put me into a lot of "firsts" for an integrated world. Whatever the playing field was, I tried to enter it fully prepared, with a positive attitude, and a smile. Whether it was football, or college, or business, I never wanted to be held back by anger or resentments. *Ugliness can destroy your heart and your faith.*

There was more controversy when Governor Frank Keating appointed me Oklahoma Secretary of Commerce. The Senate never confirmed my appointment. But I have learned to stay focused …knowing that good things will come.

I'd like to take credit for my good fortune and I *have* always worked hard, but my life is all about what miracles God has done. Through grace He has changed so many challenges into opportunities.

Maybe God has been so gracious to me because He knew I needed Him so much. You have to have faith if you have lived my life. Even during the successful times, I have been picketed and marched on. I have asked God for protection because I needed it.

My greatest blessings have been my wife of more than 50 years and three amazing children who have grown into outstanding and generous adults. I enjoy my work every day and appreciate the opportunity to be involved in my community. I sit on numerous boards and serve in many leadership positions where I'm often the only man of color in the room, except for those who serve our lunch. I shake everyone's hand when I enter the room—the fellow board members *and* the wait staff.

At the end of the day, it's me and God and I'm on my knees where I belong. I learned a long time ago that you need a good, clean heart to solve problems. Overall, I'd say that a lot of kindness has been directed my way; it's grown a grateful man.

RUSSELL M. PERRY

Owner & President, Perry Publishing and Broadcasting Company,
Former Oklahoma Secretary of Commerce, and Oklahoma Hall of Fame Inductee
Oklahoma City, OK

THEREFORE WE DO NOT LOSE HEART.
THOUGH OUTWARDLY WE ARE WASTING AWAY,
YET INWARDLY WE ARE BEING RENEWED DAY BY DAY.
FOR OUR LIGHT AND MOMENTARY TROUBLES ARE ACHIEVING FOR US AN
ETERNAL GLORY THAT FAR OUTWEIGHS THEM ALL.
SO WE FIX OUR EYES NOT ON WHAT IS SEEN,
BUT ON WHAT IS UNSEEN, SINCE WHAT IS SEEN IS TEMPORARY,
BUT WHAT IS UNSEEN IS ETERNAL.

2 CORINTHIANS 4: 16-18

We were childhood sweethearts, married for 42 years, and tethered to a baseball life. From little league to the major leagues, Bobby Murcer's love for the game never waned. In 1964, his career with the Yankees took off and the annual schedule charted our course every year. Our kids looked forward to spring training, and spending summers hanging out at major league ballparks. It seemed a normal home life.

Bobby had several memorable highlights during his days in pinstripes and was always a fan favorite, even after retiring from active play in 1983. Behind the microphone, he called Yankees games for the next 24 years. He kept fit, ran the New York Marathon, played in numerous Old Timers' Day games, and complained only when the constant travel wore him down. We always imagined this routine would take us into our golden years. But we hit a speed bump!

Life throws curveballs, and this one knocked Bobby for a loop. His 2006 brain cancer diagnosis was quickly reported in the news, bringing a legion of sports fans, rallying support from around the world. We asked for prayers and privacy as we dealt with the initial surgery and prognosis, not ready to go public with the terrifying results—a Glioblastoma Multiforme Grade 4. A million posts registered on the Yankee website…prayers and messages of hope for Bobby's recovery flooded the airwaves. Believing we could better continue, armed with all this love, prayers, and comfort, we decided to share our cancer journey with the press.

It's amazing how many blessings began to appear during those first weeks of chemotherapy and radiation, little miracles that carried so much weight, and heightened our faith. We became hyper aware of every God sign that appeared and, as Bobby rallied, the blessings continued. They boosted our faith, and replenished the strength and courage that cancer hopes to rob.

Deuteronomy 31: 6 became our mantra, *"Be strong and courageous. Do not be afraid or terrified because of them, for the Lord your God goes with you; He will never leave you nor forsake you."* It was a verse my brother Dwaine had shared as his "go to" comfort during life's most trying times. Bobby and I found our morning devotionals to be mood lifters, the vitamins we depended on to get the day started with hope and determination. Chemo treatments continued, hopefully keeping the cancer at bay, while Bobby prepared for his return to the broadcast booth in 2007.

During his final year, we wrote a book, *Yankee for Life*. In the introduction we tell how the cancer brought into focus the bigger picture of Bobby's career. We saw how the notoriety he'd achieved would bring this wider audience to witness life lessons we were experiencing. Through sharing our God-led journey, we received letters of encouragement, met wonderful families who were in treatment for the same deadly cancer, reconnected with old friends, and cherished every moment with our family and closest friends. It was a time not of fear, but of appreciation for all the blessings we still had.

After Bobby lost his battle with cancer in 2008, I discovered the above Deuteronomy scripture underlined in his Bible—it seemed to be a little PS for me to find. I trust in those words, and try to see the bigger picture that lies ahead for all of us. I also received letters from many who had a Bobby story to share, anecdotes of Bobby's kindnesses to fans, his visits to hospital patients, and letters written to ailing children. The guy I'd fallen in love with as a teen always displayed kindness and courage, though his humor and athletic talents may have eclipsed them. But during those last 18 months of his life, it was his faith and courage that took center stage.

KAY MURCER
Wife of BOBBY MURCER

New York Yankees All-Star and Broadcaster and Oklahoma Hall of Fame Inductee
Oklahoma City, OK

IN THIS WORLD YOU WILL HAVE TROUBLE.
BUT TAKE HEART! I HAVE OVERCOME THE WORLD.

JOHN 16:33

In 1991 I was involved in advising the Ukrainian government in its quest for independence from the Soviet Union. Levko Lukyanenko was one of the independence movement leaders. Mr. Lukyanenko had spent a lifetime standing up to oppression. He was imprisoned along with other dissidents by Soviet President Mikhail Gorbachev for his political criticism of the Soviet Union. After several years, President Gorbachev offered to release all political prisoners contingent upon certain conditions. Ultimately, all accepted the terms except for Levko. He stayed in prison for two years by himself as the sole prisoner in a prison designed to hold 400 inmates. He would not accept release until his freedom was unconditional.

Mr. Lukyanenko recounted this story to me and a delegation of Congressmen from the United States at a dinner during the independence elections. While eating a bowl of borscht, he told us the story without drama. The only condition placed on his release was that he would not criticize the Soviet Union once back in the public. He stayed in prison two years until this condition was non-binding. Each of us paused, amazed at this commitment to his beliefs. He felt our eyes staring at him. He looked up at us and finally made eye contact, and said, "You are Americans. Surely you would have done the same thing for freedom." The American delegation remained silent, but we could see it in each other's eyes, "I don't know what I would have done."

I think of that evening and the impact it had on my life. I remember the courage, the commitment, and the example set by Mr. Lukyanenko. What was he really saying? Why did this have such an impact on me? What was the truth to be derived?

In this life there will be difficulties. Our faith will be challenged. Many will compromise their faith. But for truth to prevail, we must be committed to its defense. Fear should not rule us in this system of things. For we are to take heart that the Lord has overcome this world. I believe this was the message that so moved my spirit that night.

To become stronger, it is imperative that we overcome strain. If we seek life, liberty, and joy, the Father cannot provide it unless we have developed the strength to maintain our faith. Oswald Chambers put it this way, "God does not give us overcoming life; he gives us life as we overcome." In the 12th chapter of 2 Corinthians, the Apostle Paul is discussing a difficulty. Jesus replies, "My grace is sufficient for you, for my power is made perfect in weakness." Paul then states, "Therefore I will boast all the more gladly about my weaknesses, so that Christ's power may rest on me. That is why, for Christ's sake, I delight in weaknesses, in insults, in hardships, in persecutions, in difficulties. For when I am weak, then I am strong." Trust in the Lord for His strength.

As I face the problems generated by this world, I am at peace. For in my purpose, I have opportunity. Yet in my difficulties, I have the answer to fear. For when difficulties seem overwhelming, I know that Christ has overcome the world. It is only my faith then that is in question. And the question of my faith is totally under my control. I have but to commit to the truth and defend it, even if it means being in prison alone for two years. God will see us through. My fear is overcome by my weakness because in my weakness, God's strength makes me whole. His power is perfect.

MARC NUTTLE

International Lawyer, Author, and former Presidential Advisor
Norman, OK

I WILL SING AND MAKE MUSIC WITH ALL MY SOUL.

PSALM 108:1A

I don't remember not singing.

I sang while chopping cotton …to the annoyance of my brother. My sister led the way, singing alto to my soprano.

I sang at church, in our living room, at school.

As I grew, my audience expanded to weddings and even funerals.

In high school, I graduated to musical theater and contests. College was a huge step up in training and experience. There, I discovered exceptional teaching and intense competition.

One day I knew music was more than something I did …it was a huge part of who I was. Singing was my gift—my passion. It was also my *choice* as to how to use my voice. Was it a hobby, or a disciplined life work, that set up a future that I had never imagined in the cotton fields of my youth? I learned from my voice professor, Florence Birdwell, that music could indeed be a life and not just a love.

Thanks to inspiring teachers and a supportive family, I was dead set on chasing the dream of performing on Broadway. Determined? Yes. Comfortable? No. But with no hesitation, I dedicated myself not just to singing but to the joy of communicating through music.

One cold morning when the bright dot on the Oklahoma horizon had just begun to spread its pink light, I boarded a flight to New York City by myself. I cried all the way. *Was I doing the right thing? Could I make it? Would a career be worth the sacrifice of not living near home, surrounded by family? Would the East Coast ever be anything like the warm friendliness of the Heartland?*

After months in tiny apartments with too many girlfriends, wild experiences on the subway system, and cold auditions, success met my efforts. I found work as a professional singer.

Today, several major Broadway leads, Tony nominations, and a Tony Award, are behind me. And, more importantly, I've managed to share it with my husband, and children. It's not always easy with eight shows a week, getting home late at night, little-to-no vacation time during the run of a show, and very few non-working holidays. But the privilege of performing always fills me with gratitude. One scene in particular put it all in perspective.

I was singing the role of "Clara" in *The Light in the Piazza* on Broadway, when the cast was informed that Betty Comden was very ill and unable to come to the theater to hear this new show. Betty was a hero of mine. She was one-half of the musical-comedy duo Comden and Green, who provided lyrics, libretti, and screenplays to some of the most beloved and successful Hollywood musicals and Broadway shows of the 20th century.

A few of us went to her home and sang the incredible music from "Piazza" to this musical icon. In that moment, I realized anew the importance of music. As my voice carried the music and words of the talented Adam Guettel and Clara's amazing love story, I was moved to tears. What grace to be a conduit of such a message …to be a stream of communication …connecting humans with each other and the God who is beyond, yet in, our humanity. For me, music is a form of love that is fulfilling in a way that nothing else is.

I've performed those songs before thousands of audiences and every time it is meaningful. But whether it's for a crowd of a thousand or one, like Ms. Comden, the gift is the ability to be the vocal instrument of the words and the music.

Betty Comden wrote the lyrics to a song called, "Make Someone Happy." Its message is simple …that nothing in life matters as much as learning to love. To sing that, to live that, is my greatest honor.

KELLI O'HARA

Professional Singer/Actress, Tony Award Winner,
and Oklahoma Hall of Fame Inductee
Elk City, OK

PRACTICE
COMES FIRST IN RELIGION,
NOT THEORY OR DOGMA. AND
CHRISTIAN PRACTICE
IS NOT EXHAUSTED
IN OUTWARD DEEDS.
THESE ARE THE FRUITS
NOT THE ROOTS.

THOMAS KELLY

LISTEN, MY BELOVED BRETHREN:
DID NOT GOD CHOOSE THE POOR OF THIS WORLD TO BE RICH
IN FAITH AND HEIRS OF THE KINGDOM WHICH HE PROMISED
TO THOSE WHO LOVE HIM?

JAMES 2:5

The Apostle James could have easily written this verse about my dad, John Gregg.

Dad was poor. He and Mom were tenant farmers in rural Oklahoma during the Dust Bowl and Great Depression. He never owned the land we farmed. He had an eighth grade education. Yet, this humble man taught me all I would ever need to know about faith, charity, wealth, and the hard work that yields these treasures.

I was raised in a Christian home by parents who prayed, read the Bible, and took us to church. My siblings and I were taught the importance of honoring God in word and deed. I realize, now, the most valuable teaching came from those *deeds*, especially regarding lessons of charity.

My father was the most generous man I have ever known, despite our lack of material abundance. He gave freely and frequently of his time, energy, and yes *even money*. John Gregg was the first to run to the aid of a neighbor. In the 1930s and 1940s of my childhood, there were an abundance of neighbors in need.

Understand, poverty and fear are frequent bedfellows. My child's mind often struggled with fear about our scarcity of the simplest necessities: shoes, pencils, notebooks for school. So, watching my father give away our last dime, literally, *not* figuratively, would strike terror into my little heart. Sometimes, I boldly challenged him, "Why are we giving that coin away?" His response was always a reflection of Christ, *"Give and it will be given to you…for with the measure you use, it will be measured to you."* In others words, when you give freely, your bread eventually comes back to you buttered. No one could quote scripture better than my dad and I doubt anyone lived it more fully. Somehow, some way, John Gregg always worked to provide for our family with sweat and initiative.

One would think that a lifetime of poverty, despite an incredible work ethic and hard labor, might have planted seeds of bitterness in Dad's heart. Within me, anger sometimes befriended the fear I felt about our lack. Perhaps sensing this or perhaps by the divine presence of the Holy Spirit, Dad changed the course of my life in one brief history lesson. I was eight years old; I tagged along with him that day, while he was running errands in town. I liked picking out the sacks of feed for our livestock because Mom would use the floral fabric of those sacks to sew my dresses. That day, as we drove through Enid, Oklahoma, in Dad's jalopy of a car, he pulled over to the curb in front of the Carnegie Library building. "What are we doing here?" I wondered. Dad came around to the passenger side of the car, opened the door, took my hand, and walked with me up the steps to the front of the library. There, he told me the story of Andrew Carnegie's life. Carnegie had been raised in poverty, then became wealthy by building a business in the steel industry. His life's goal was to give away all of his money before he died, which he did in the form of public libraries built in towns and villages across the United States. At the conclusion, Dad looked deep into my eyes and said, "Always respect the wealthy, because the wealthy give back." I was stunned and, simultaneously, *driven*. My dad lit a flame that burned like fire in my belly motivating me to reach for a life I had never before imagined.

Dad's lessons were two-fold that day. He gave me permission to aspire to become wealthy, despite our poverty. And, he deeply etched on my heart the obligation to give back. After all, *"to those whom much is given, much is required."*

In time, I was blessed with great abundance through business ownership; bread does come back buttered. I had to rely on the work ethic instilled in me and the journey required great leaps of faith. Over the years, I have never forgotten Dad's story about Carnegie. I have often wondered if I might still be in poverty had I not received that lesson.

Every day, I pray that the seeds of Dad's generosity, charity, and hard work have been cast on fertile ground with me. May Dad, Mom and Jesus look down from Heaven and see my life as a crop that has yielded *thirty, sixty, even a hundred times that which was planted.*

MO ANDERSON

Vice Chairman of the Board and former President & CEO, Keller Williams Realty International
and Oklahoma Hall of Fame Inductee
Waukomis/Edmond, OK

FOR WHERE TWO OR THREE ARE GATHERED TOGETHER IN MY NAME,
THERE AM I IN THE MIDST OF THEM.

MATTHEW 18:20

The workplace often seems an intersection of ambition and competition, of opportunity and disappointment, of long hours and the pursuit of financial reward. Rarely is it considered a safe harbor where faith is strengthened or "loving your neighbor" is practical.

Perhaps that is why meeting Frank McPherson had such a profound impact on my spiritual life. Frank grew up in Stilwell, Oklahoma in modest circumstances and worked his way to an engineering degree at Oklahoma State University. He then went to work for Kerr-McGee Corporation, a multi-national energy and chemical company headquartered in Oklahoma City. He climbed the corporate ladder through a myriad of assignments and positions over several decades. Ultimately, he became the company's CEO, succeeding legendary oilman and community leader, Dean A. McGee.

The leadership team Frank assembled included me. After several years practicing law and a stint in state government, joining Kerr-McGee seemed like a great opportunity. While there were several title changes for me in the ensuing years my jobs could all be described in one word, "troubleshooter." There seemed to be no end to the legal, regulatory, environmental, and political and public relations issues we faced in our businesses around the country and indeed around the world.

But Frank was rock solid. It did not take long to see why. He was buoyed by a Christian faith stronger than I had ever seen in a business context. Never overbearing or condescending, he simply set an example. Daily devotions, prayer, support for colleagues, and a confidence "that all things work together for those who love the Lord," made him a role model for many, including me.

Unobtrusive, but always ready to share his faith, Frank became a mentor to me. As business related challenges cascaded around us, he counseled to focus on the things we could control and ask God to give us strength for the journey. His calm, faith-based approach saw us all through many sleepless nights and troubled waters.

Frank retired from the company and then three years later, I did. I was unsure how our relationship and friendship would continue. He had his life to live and mine was going a different direction, ultimately leading me to the presidency of Oklahoma City University.

One day Frank called to suggest that he would like to bring a young church friend named Steve Garder, a dentist, to begin a weekly Bible Study in my office at OCU. He related that he felt a call to start these individual small group study sessions to stoke the fires of our faith. He was doing the same with several groups.

For the next ten years we met early every Friday morning. Frank furnished the study material and we held each other accountable to be prepared. In the midst of a busy, hectic new life at the University, this weekly meeting became central to my spiritual life.

Although I had always gone to church regularly, Frank brought a new dimension for living a Christian life in a real world context. Studying, sharing, and praying together on a regular basis was the booster shot I needed.

When I have tried to express my appreciation to Frank for all he has meant to my faith journey, he has simply said, "If you want to thank me, find two more friends and study the Bible with them." So I have. It is the surest way I know to see that Frank's Christian legacy will endure and perhaps inspire others to do the same.

Tom J. McDaniel

President, American Fidelity Foundation, former President, Oklahoma City University, Attorney, and Oklahoma Hall of Fame Inductee
Coalgate/Alva/Oklahoma City, OK

CONSIDER IT PURE JOY, MY BROTHERS AND SISTERS,
WHENEVER YOU FACE TRIALS OF MANY KINDS,
BECAUSE YOU KNOW THAT THE TESTING OF YOUR FAITH PRODUCES
PERSEVERANCE. LET PERSEVERANCE FINISH ITS WORK
SO THAT YOU MAY BE MATURE AND COMPLETE,
NOT LACKING ANYTHING.

JAMES 1:2-4

My hands flipped the bed sheets up, smoothed them out, and the pink pillow landed on top. John, my husband, stood in the doorway, "Noma, why are you making their beds? You work hard all day in court; those two girls don't appreciate it. Why do you bother?"

"I don't even know," I answered. "But my mother made my bed, and I'm going to make theirs."

The busy tidy lives of my attorney-husband and my life as a trial judge on the district court bench had been turned upside down by two young girls.

A few years earlier, in California, my younger sister and her husband had been foster parents to the girls and then adopted them in 2003. The girls were seven and eight years old at that time. They had already been in five or six foster homes. Their biological mother was in prison. But my sister and her husband were able to legally get custody of them. John and I were supportive.

In 2004 my sister was diagnosed with breast cancer and lived about 2 ½ years. Six weeks following her death, her husband committed suicide. And there were the girls.

We were stunned! I couldn't even grieve the loss of my sister because of the chaos, and I was responsible for making order of it. What was to become of the girls who, only recently adopted, now had no parents? The court was ready to send them back to a children's shelter. Should my husband and I take them?

We were middle aged and had no children. We were career oriented—with two cats.

We prayed for direction. We already knew the answer. Nothing about it was easy.

Out we flew to California and a tangle of legal problems. My sister and spouse had died without making any plans—no wills, no notes about the daughters, no lists of people to contact, not even information on how to stop the milk delivery.

Tons of red tape surrounded two adopted children. But we were determined to cut through the entanglements and keep them in the family.

After working wonders within the California legal system, we managed to pack the girls' bags and bring them home. We enrolled the girls in school; by the grace of God we kept them there. We took them to church; if they didn't go to the worship service with us, they worked in the church nursery. Nobody was happy. We just did our best.

That is all history today. From the minute we made our decision to help the girls, God placed the most incredible people in our lives to make it possible. While the road was bumpy, at times even hazardous, the love and encouragement from our faith family was the foundation beneath our feet. Even strangers we met in California found a way to bless us.

There is no happily ever after to this story, but there are victories. Today, both girls have high school diplomas. One won art scholarships to major universities throughout America. Both have attended and one completed college. The girls are living independently. I am proud of them.

I grew up attending a little country church on a dirt road in rural Indiana. God was real to me in those early years, but never did I suspect He would call me to play this role in life. I wasn't prepared in many ways, but in other ways, God had equipped me to handle many of the details. Few others could have navigated the legal maze that allowed us to keep the girls out of institutional care.

The small miracles have been numerous, but the big miracle is this: two beautiful children who began with seemingly nothing on their side, now, have a chance at a better life. For many years they had a safe home, material needs provided, and exposure to church and community. They know there is a God and He loves them unconditionally. My husband and I continue to pray for them every day.

When I think back to those mornings when I felt overwhelmed and inadequate to handle the responsibility of these children, I remain grateful. God is faithful and when I wasn't positive of the right thing to do, I trusted God enough to just do the next thing …even if it was something so simple as to make their beds.

NOMA GURICH

Justice, Supreme Court of Oklahoma
Oklahoma City, OK

BE STRONG AND OF GOOD COURAGE;
DO NOT BE AFRAID, NOR BE DISMAYED,
FOR THE LORD YOUR GOD IS WITH YOU WHEREVER YOU GO.

JOSHUA 1:9

It was a dark evening. I was in a foul mood. We were all eating dinner around the kitchen table. I pushed back from my plate and walked down the hall with my head low. My wife, Cathy, followed me. "Phil. You're so down—what's the matter?"

"What's the *matter?*" I said. "I don't have a job, I don't know if I have a future. I don't know how I'm going to pay our mortgage or what I'm going to do about anything."

We stared at each other. Then Cathy said, "Is that all?" She continued staring me down. "Walk back in there and look at those three beautiful, healthy, kids sitting at the table in our home. We've got the most important things."

And surely we did. That was one of many grace moments in my life when God was real at a level deeper than the circumstances. I knew we would be okay.

Amazingly, that was the beginning of a new career for me—from law to business. Today, Cathy and I are blessed with businesses that impact thousands of people around the world. One of our companies is Delaware Resources Group. We had no idea that with faith, starting DRG would result in its growth into a family-owned nationally recognized defense contracting firm with more than 600 employees and 55 locations globally. Our mantra is "profit with a purpose," enabling us beyond our dreams to give back to church and community and begin El Sistema, an afterschool program based on social change through music touching the lives of over 220 underserved inner city children and their families. God certainly works in mysterious ways we cannot understand unless we trust in Him and our faith.

Our children have grown into beautiful, bright, caring adults. They have found their paths to success and we remain a close family. Life has been great …but then another "dark evening."

Almost overnight, at the age of 61, I became partially paralyzed by what was diagnosed as Guillain-Barre syndrome, a rare nerve disorder. It began with the sense that my feet were on fire; and, in a matter of hours, I began to lose feeling in my body. In no time, my health became critical and I lost the ability to walk.

This time I didn't need Cathy to remind me of my blessings, we had been living in gratitude for years. Now, we learned to live in faith. The scripture from Joshua 1:9 became our mantra, repeated every morning: "Have I not commanded you? Be strong and of good courage; do not be afraid, nor be dismayed, for the Lord your God is with you wherever you go."

My health stabilized and I continue to work on my recovery. I have learned the challenges facing disabled persons. It has enhanced my faith and changed the way I look at each and every person, to appreciate their stories and the gifts each of us bring, regardless of circumstance.

None of us know for sure what tomorrow brings …a job loss, a health decline, something worse? But we can be grateful for what we have today. We can live with *courage and strength* because God is with us.

Is that all?

It's enough.

PHIL G. BUSEY, SR.

Chairman & CEO, The Busey Group of Companies
Oklahoma City, OK

WE CAN MAKE OUR PLANS,
BUT THE LORD DETERMINES OUR STEPS.
PROVERBS 16:9

I like to have a plan. When I became a single mother, my plan was to become the "best mother" ever! Raising my only child, a daughter, was going to be a challenge under any circumstances, but raising her in the affluent community of Edmond was going to be doubly hard. When she reached the age of 11, it became apparent that she was a girl of "privilege," so I set out to find ways to help her serve others. My plan was for us to do volunteer work at the City Rescue Mission, which was nothing like it is today, located on South Robinson Street in Oklahoma City.

I made the call and was told that we could serve in the kitchen the following day. As we walked through the door, we were greeted with smells of body odor, cooking food, and smelly feet. There was no air conditioning, just large fans circulating the odors through the room. Immediately, my daughter began to dry heave and to cover her nose with her tee shirt as tears rolled down her cheeks. I, the "best mother" ever, was appalled! Surely, I had taught her better! After a lecture in the restroom, we finished our task in the kitchen and returned home. I was haunted by her behavior and promptly called the "Mission" to see what else they had for us to do. Long story short, we became a part of their team and helped to host Bible clubs on Saturdays. It was during these Bible clubs that God introduced me to a three-year-old boy that would be the catalyst for changing the direction of our lives.

Miguel was not the boy I would have chosen to become a part of our lives. He reminded me of Mowgli in *The Jungle Book;* he bit, kicked, hit, and wanted no part of any Bible lesson. As time passed, he began to form a relationship with my daughter and began asking us to take him home after club time. We discovered that he lived in the Shidler-Wheeler community of southeast Oklahoma City. He was one of five children being raised by a single mother with little means of support. Miguel eventually found out that I was a teacher. He told me that he could not read and let me know that it was *my job* to teach him! He was very persistent. Each week he would wait until club time was over, crawl into my car, and begin the lecture about it being my duty to teach him how to read. What he didn't realize was that I had never taught anyone to read before because I was a high school English teacher.

Plan #2: I was finally worn down about the reading, so I decided to tell Miguel that I would teach him to read if he could come live with us. Now, there was no way that his mother, who did not even know my name, was going to let him live with us, right? I would ask. She would say, "No," and that would be the end of it. Well, here is where Proverbs 16:9 comes into play. You see, I had a plan, but God had a better one. Miguel's mother said "Yes." And, on a wintery Sunday afternoon, I brought home a seven-year-old Mexican boy to live with my now 14-year-old daughter and me. Miguel lived with us for three years, and during that time, Miguel taught me about a world I never knew existed. He introduced me to a community that was underserved, that knew nothing of God and His promises, and that found their hope and support from the local elementary school.

God used Miguel to introduce me to a forgotten community whom I have come to love and serve for the past 25 years. God used a three-year-old boy to teach my daughter and me how to really "love our neighbors as ourselves," and how to let God direct our steps. Through Miguel Elizalde, God created FaithWorks of the Inner City where I now serve as founder and executive director. FaithWorks serves 200 families living in the Shidler-Wheeler community through after school programs, a pre-school, a church, job training, housing programs, and community development. By following God's plan instead of my own, my life and my daughter's life have been blessed and enriched with relationships, experiences, and miracles. And Miguel… he continues to be a part of our family. He walked me down the aisle at my daughter's wedding. My grandchildren call him "tio," meaning uncle. He is a FaithWorks' employee, mentoring and encouraging children who are growing up as he did.

… Oh, and that "privileged girl," she is also a FaithWork's employee!

SALLY GOIN

Teacher and Founder & Executive Director, FaithWorks
Oklahoma City, OK

SO I WILL BLESS YOU AS LONG AS I LIVE;

PSALM 63:4

Searing fever and tremendous body aches awakened me in a Jerusalem hotel room. It was one of the most important days of my life, the dedication of a library wing of Ben-Gurion University named in honor of my father. I was deathly ill …so weak I could hardly move.

Nothing would keep me from delivering my prepared remarks at this event that included the highest dignitaries of Israel. My father had died two years before, but this was his dream. A European Jew, he had immigrated to Oklahoma at the age of 18 and started a scrap metal business at 21. This was the result of his dedication to hard work and the opportunities of his adopted homeland.

My entire Oklahoma family was with me for the ceremony. I dressed and went downstairs for breakfast. In the lobby, I fainted and the hotel doctor documented a fever of 107 degrees and put me to bed. After a shot and some pills, I handed my written remarks to my wife and accepted that this severe illness was beyond my control. I slept.

That beautiful day in the Holy Land, while the Israelis and Americans honored my father, I believe that I died. My spirit left my body. I saw myself below on the hotel bed. There was no pain, no sounds. I heard the voice of G-d and answered Him. I don't remember the tone of G-d's voice or any visual appearance, but I pleaded for my life. I told G-d there were many things unfinished in my life and I asked to go back. Then G-d asked me to do something and I promised that I would. While I will never divulge the details of that promise, it is something that I attempt to do daily. It has influenced every moment of my life since that time.

When the family returned later that afternoon, I awakened, completely healed. I wasn't just better; I felt great. There was no remnant of illness, no tiredness, just exuberance at the Holy encounter.

44

That "dream" was stored in my private memory for many years. Seven years later, in an unlikely series of circumstances, my family and I happened to visit a children's museum in Michigan. That visit began the most amazing journey: the creation of a children's museum in my hometown of Seminole, Oklahoma, named for my wife: The Jasmine Moran Children's Museum.

I created a board of trustees for the museum of total newcomers to boards, fund raising, and museums. They were educators and young moms. We were so naïve. But the same G-d who spoke to me in Jerusalem, directed every step of this effort. Miracle after miracle occurred. Today, more than one-million visitors have benefitted from a visit to this museum.

Yes, this project was part of my promise to G-d.

Each morning, I'm reminded of the wonder that is G-d. I'm a very practical man, not prone to dreams or fantasy. I served in a top secret unit of the U.S. Air Force in England during the Korean War, where I met my wife of over 58 years. I have worked for over 60 years in the oil business. Father to three, grandfather to six, past president of many organizations in my community and state, I'm the last person who expected a personal encounter with the G-d.

Why would He speak to me? Why would I be blessed with these opportunities?

I wonder. I accept. I give thanks.

MELVIN MORAN

Owner, Moran Oil Enterprises, Founder, Jasmine Moran Children's Museum,
and Oklahoma Hall of Fame Inductee
Seminole, OK

WELL, I HAD TO LEARN HOW TO
TRUST THE LORD.
MY FAITH MUSCLES GREW.
JUST LIKE YOU'RE EXERCISING
YOUR MUSCLES AND THEY MAY
BE SORE FOR A WHILE, BUT THEY
BECOME STRONGER WITH EXERCISE.

**FAITH GROWS
WITH EXERCISE.**
YOU SEE GOD
WORK MIRACLES.

BILL BRIGHT, COWETA
Founder, Campus Crusade for Christ and
Oklahoma Hall of Fame Inductee

WE WILL BLESS THE LORD AT ALL TIMES
AND HIS PRAISE SHALL CONTINUOUSLY BE IN OUR MOUTH.

PSALM 34:1

I am old enough to honestly see and understand the many blessings that God has placed in my life. The first blessing was to be born to Lucious and Jessie Selmon. My dad was a sharecropper; his work in the field started at sunrise and ended at sunset. My mother took care of the house, washed the clothes, cooked the meals, worked in the garden, and watched over nine children, the last three being Lucious, Lee Roy, and myself. In the evening, after all work was done, they would sit us down in the front room and talk to us about God and the Bible and how it inspired and protected them. We were taught to pray, listen, work, and be thankful for our blessings. Of course, I didn't always see my blessings. We were living in a four-room wood frame house without air conditioning, television, or a family car. Riding to church behind a mule in the family wagon did not pump up the ego. But as I have grown older, the times spent in that old wagon with all my brothers and sisters have become treasured memories. Sometimes my parents would drive us into town, each one of us in possession of our own spoon. They would stop and buy a gallon of ice cream and we would sit and eat in that wagon, thinking there could be no greater blessing on this Earth.

Inside our small rural church the blessings flowed. The Bible was taught and shared. Spirituals were sung and prayers from bent knees were lifted up to God. Families gathered, children played, food was served, and a hope in a brighter tomorrow discussed. My brothers and I sat in the middle of the church. Men sat on one side, women on the other, and children in the middle. I still remember the quick, sharp glances from my mother which sometimes proclaimed that we were being too squirmy or inattentive. We sat straight up with eyes forward in immediate response. A special blessing was the Sunday when I, along with six other children my age, was taken across the road to a large farm pond and baptized by the deacons of the church. That blessing still holds fast to my heart, for even then I felt as though I was a part of something eternally big.

God blessed me to see and grow through the civil rights movement. My parents had always taught us to love and respect everyone regardless of color. The civil rights movement touched even rural McIntosh County, and there were days we shed rivers of tears for the hurt and hurting. Schools were eventually integrated in eastern Oklahoma; the three of us were introduced to football by Eufaula High School Coach Paul Bell, a man who blessed our family beyond measure. We went on to play at the University of Oklahoma. Coach Barry Switzer led the team in such a way that we became family; each and every one are some of my greatest blessings in life to this day.

In addition to winning a few football games, I met my wife Kathryn at OU. We have six lovely children. We struggled at times. There was a transition period that came when football was over. I looked for a new place in the world. But through it all, we sat and talked to our children about God and the Bible. They were taken to church at an early age. They were baptized and taught to pray. They were taught to be thankful for people, their circumstances, and the blessings of God, our Father. I wanted to make sure the circle would not be broken.

Over our mantel there is a simple wooden sign that reads, "We will bless the Lord at all times and His Praise shall continuously be in our mouth." Life won't always be easy. But praise forever remains. Just look beyond the surface and see the expansive blue sky, the tallgrass prairies, and the deep red soil, the highest tree, and the smallest bird. They all sing His name.

DEWEY SELMON, PH.D.

University of Oklahoma Football Great, NFL Football Player,
and Oklahoma Sports Hall of Fame Inductee
Eufaula/Norman, OK

FOR WE ARE GOD'S MASTERPIECE.
HE HAS CREATED US ANEW IN CHRIST JESUS,
SO WE CAN DO THE GOOD THINGS HE PLANNED FOR US LONG AGO.

EPHESIANS 2:10

One of the questions I get asked most frequently is "How do I know what my purpose is?" Or "How do I know which road I am supposed to take?"

From the time I was ten years old, when my dreams of being an Olympic gymnast were dashed, I started asking myself these same questions. Every year I would start a new journey or a new hobby in hopes of discovering my purpose or finding something I was passionate enough about to make it my life's calling. I knew deep in my heart God had gifted me with something that He was preparing me for even if that gift was not yet apparent.

As a matter of fact, He has given each one of us a unique gift that some of us have not even unwrapped yet. Many of us are living or longing for someone else's gift. We are walking down someone else's road.

Living someone else's journey.

The key is to walk the path God has mapped out especially for you.
Sometimes it is barely lit.
Sometimes you cannot see beyond the next step.
But you just put one foot in front of the other.
And keep walking.

Sometimes the door is not wide open. It's simply unlocked.
And so you walk through it.
But never should you need to bang a door down.
Or walk down a road that is blocked.

There are no actual directions or bright yellow signs saying "Turn Left" or "Make a U turn".

It is as if your heart is a magnetic compass always drawing you towards the path you are to walk down.

So while your head may be filled with doubts, fears, and internal criticisms as to whether to go or to stay...the answer is:

First Stand Still.

Simply so you can listen.

And feel.

And have your compass reset.

Then watch the magnetic pull of that arrow on your heart's compass.

Which direction is it pulling you?

Which door is it pointing towards?

Which path is it shedding a little light on?

When you are still,

Not only does it give your compass a moment to reset,

It makes you intentional about listening closely.

About seeing things clearly.

And mostly about feeling the true pull of your heart.

Not the pull of someone else.

We are pulled all day.

In all directions.

Every day.

Month after month.

Year after year.

So much so that we no longer listen to our own heart's desires.

The ones that God put in there.

Stop going to everyone else for answers.
To social media.
To blogs.
To quizzes and tests.
Asking everyone what to do.
Asking for wisdom is one thing.
But listening to the ONE thing that only you can know is another.
Your heart.

If you stand still.
It will get quiet enough
that you may rediscover
an answer that is buried
yet has been there all along.

God gave you certain desires.
He put them in your heart.
Discover the direction the arrow is pointing and then take a simple step.
And keep following it.
Even when the road bends.
It is better than any road map you will ever find.

JILL DONOVAN

Attorney, Speaker, Writer, and Founder, Rustic Cuff
Tulsa, OK

INSTEAD, BE KIND TO EACH OTHER,
TENDERHEARTED, FORGIVING ONE ANOTHER,
JUST AS GOD THROUGH CHRIST HAS FORGIVEN YOU.

EPHESIANS 4:32

It was still pitch black that spring morning when I got into the car. My mood was just as dark.

Oklahoma was home for only four months, but it was hard not to be impressed by the friendly nature of its people. However, that morning I was grumbling to myself about Oklahoma's "Bible Belt" tradition because weeks earlier I had committed to attend a 7:00 a.m. prayer breakfast preceded by a *6:15 a.m.* prayer reception hosted by the justices of the Supreme Court of Oklahoma.

I was told the prayer breakfast was a powerful spiritual event. My unspoken motivation for accepting the invitation was less noble: my company had a major case pending before the Supreme Court and I thought it might be worth getting up so early to meet the justices and others in an informal setting. But the morning of the event, I grumbled to myself the entire drive downtown to what was then called the Myriad Convention Center.

People were smiling and hospitable the moment I walked in the reception room. The director of the host, Christian Business Men's Committee, welcomed me and immediately introduced me to what seemed like dozens of city and state leaders. Before I could meet any of the Supreme Court justices, the group was lead in a prayer and we were quickly escorted to the mayor's prayer breakfast in the convention center's primary hall.

When I looked out from the head table, I was stunned. Row after row of tables were filled with people even at that early hour. I wish I could say I remember the keynote speech that followed. I can't. What occurred shortly after the breakfast is unforgettable. The day was April 19, 1995.

It was about 8:45 a.m. when I drove past the Alfred P. Murrah Federal Building on the way to my office located two blocks north. When I arrived at my office, my assistant reminded me of my 9:00 a.m. meeting scheduled to be in our general counsel's office. Still whining from getting up early, I asked her to shift the meeting to my office because I was already "so tired."

The meeting in my office just began when we were literally knocked off our chairs. It would be much later before we learned what happened: the Murrah Building had been bombed, creating the most horrific act of terrorism in United States history.

What unfolded was transformational for America, for Oklahoma City, and for me. The story of Oklahomans' response to the bombing is better chronicled elsewhere. For me, the depth of human hate was laid bare. Still, I'm blessed because God also allowed me witness—up close—examples of overwhelming human love from so many Oklahomans whose selflessness lifted neighbors, an entire community, and a nation.

God also soon revealed He had forgiven my petty, self-centered attitude that started the day. The general counsel's office where we were to have met had a large window facing south, toward the Murrah Building. The force of the bombing shattered the large window and projected shards of glass in every direction. Large pieces of glass by the dozens were stuck in the walls of the office, from floor to ceiling. Clearly, we had been spared by not meeting there. Decades later, "live to forgive" is the Lord's whisper that haunts me still.

DAVE LOPEZ

Retired Officer at SBC Communications
and Former Oklahoma Secretary of Commerce and Secretary of State
Oklahoma City, OK

"FOR I KNOW THE PLANS I HAVE FOR YOU," DECLARES THE LORD,
"PLANS TO PROSPER YOU AND NOT TO HARM YOU,
PLANS TO GIVE YOU HOPE AND A FUTURE."

JEREMIAH 28:11

Some of us are fortunate to know that we are called to a specific purpose from a young age. I was one. As a fifth-generation Oklahoman growing up on a farm outside of Pond Creek, one of my earliest memories was telling my pediatrician, the only person in medicine I knew, that I was going to be a doctor. He encouraged that precocious, but determined, four-year-old to become a nurse, even offering me a job when I grew up.

Whether forcing my little sister to play "doll hospital" or convincing classmates that they really wanted to take anatomy/physiology so my small rural high school and amazing science teacher would offer it, I stayed committed to this commitment to become a physician. However, even with a strong calling, as most of us learn at some point, the path is often not straight or easy even when we are actively seeking the will of God.

Throughout high school and college, I was solely focused on the medicine track. I thought I had done all of the right things—studied hard, made good grades, and pursued clinical shadowing opportunities. However, a person close to the medical school told me that I really needed some research exposure to get in the medical school door. This led me to apply to the Fleming Scholar program at the Oklahoma Medical Research Foundation (OMRF), at the time the only summer research experience for high school/college students. I applied as a driven high school student only to be told "no" and to try back the following year after some college research exposure. I then applied again after a stellar freshman year at Oklahoma Baptist University to only be told "no", again not even getting an interview, because I did not have enough research experience.

OK, at this point, I had to admit to being a bit more than frustrated because wasn't I applying to the Fleming program to get this research experience?

However, I was very persistent and was determined to find a research experience that would lead to this coveted Fleming scholarship. I was a chemistry major, even though biology was the dominant major for pre-med students. This decision was based upon my dad's advice that I needed a back-up plan for a real job. I was looking for a chemistry experiment to do on my assigned animal for zoology. After several days of playing with my least favorite animals of all—snakes—I wanted to sway the professor to not assign me a snake but to give me fish to care for and experiment with for an entire semester. I anxiously went to the board to find my animal assignment. Thankfully, I was not assigned a snake. Instead I received two large black tarantulas. After some investigation, I put those spiders in what had been my make up bag and drove to Stillwater to learn how to milk tarantulas from an OSU professor. I then tried to isolate toxins from these new strains, which might help stimulate nerve growth.

Although the toxins were never useful for treatment of human disease, that research experience did get me an interview and selection as a Fleming Scholar. That long-awaited exposure forged my passion for clinical research focused on the original OMRF mission, "that more may live longer, healthier lives" and inspires me still, 29 years later as I remain at OMRF and the OU Health Sciences Center. This is where I serve in leadership roles focused on a new calling to improve the health of Oklahomans and to help mentor the next generation of Oklahoma physicians and scientists.

Of course, many other challenges have occurred since those earliest experiment days, most of which did not have such a profound or positive outcome. However, this early journey helped me understand that although we have a call and are working to follow God's plan, sometimes the path to that plan is not what we expect and during those times we are called to just "Trust in the Lord with all thine heart and lean not unto our own understanding, in all our ways acknowledge him and he will make straight our paths" (Proverbs 3:5-6), even when our paths don't seem straight to us.

JUDITH A. JAMES, MD, PH.D.

Vice President of Clinical Affairs and
Chair, Arthritis and Clinical Immunology Department,
Oklahoma Medical Research Foundation and
Professor of Medicine and Associate Vice Provost for Clinical and Translational Science,
University of Oklahoma Health Sciences Center
Pond Creek/Oklahoma City, OK

WHATEVER YOU WISH THAT OTHERS WOULD DO TO YOU, DO SO TO THEM.

MATTHEW 7:12

Growing up in the delightful southwest Oklahoma town of Hobart, I had a wild imagination. I played football by myself in our front yard until dark, conducted circuses using elm-tree branches as giraffes, and presented one-man musical shows with mother's thick front-room curtains separating me from the appreciative make-believe "audience."

We were certainly free to dream in the 1950s. And I had plenty of aspirations. But I have lived a life way beyond anything I ever conjured. I never imagined that I would grow up to direct the best event in college basketball—the NCAA tournament—and then direct the best event in college football—the College Football Playoff.

In the quiet moments when I allow myself to speculate about why I have been so lucky, I keep coming back to Matthew 7:12. Everyone knows those magical words: "Whatever you wish that others would do to you, do so to them."

I believe in keeping a simple life and have always tried to live by that wonderful Golden Rule.

In sports and in life, we sometimes make things too complicated. Instead, we only need to keep it simple: block, tackle, shoot, and rebound. And treat others the way we want to be treated.

Oh, and let the giraffes roam free.

BILL HANCOCK

Executive Director, College Football Playoff, Former Director, NCAA Final Four,
Former Director, Bowl Championship Series, and Oklahoma Hall of Fame Inductee
Hobart, OK/Prairie Village, KS

WHATEVER YOU DO, DO YOUR WORK HEARTILY, AS FOR THE LORD RATHER THAN FOR MEN.

COLOSSIANS 3:23

Latrine duty? That was the task I had been given at Camp Cal-Ka-Lin. My nine-year-old heart sank low when I heard the news. What an awful and humiliating assignment.

As a young Camp Fire Girl in Vinita, Oklahoma, I could hardly wait for summer camp. This was my one week of fun, singing songs, participating in skits, taking nature hikes, cooking over an open fire, sleeping under the stars, and feeling like part of something great.

Now, I had this bum assignment: not tent set-up, wood gathering, cooking, cleaning …but latrine duty. It was because I was at the tail end of the list of girls. Because my last name began with "W", along with another camper, Christy, whose last name also began with "W", we got the last and seemingly worst task.

Christy and I looked at each other with a somewhat embarrassed glance. Then, Christy started to giggle and my mind started racing with possibilities. Soon, we both stood taller. If this was our task, then we were going to give it our best effort and have fun in the process. No complaints!

Here's what we faced: no indoor plumbing was available, so each campsite had a terracotta 12" square pipe that had been installed over a hole dug into the ground. A toilet lid was given to each campsite along with burlap, twine, and lime powder, which was to be sprinkled into the pipe after each use. We wrapped the burlap around the trees for privacy, and strung twine between trees to hold the toilet paper, then added a washing station. We poked a hole into a large used coffee can and found a small twig as a plug to hold water for hand washing. Additionally, we cut a hole into a bar of soap and tied it next to the water can. To complete the washing station, a roll of paper towels was tied to the twine line next to the coffee can. If Martha Stewart had been famous back then, this would have rivaled anything she could have built.

I don't remember the other girls being especially impressed, but Christy and I knew that we had done an amazing job.

In hindsight, this seems like such a simple event. But it says a lot about the important lessons I learned growing up in a small town in Oklahoma. Those lessons of faith, humility, and determination have served me well in all areas of my life.

Colossians 3:23 states, "Whatever you do, do your work heartily, as for the Lord rather than for men."

I have always felt an inner calling to do my best. It wasn't about winning an award or making the best grade or getting that promotion, but rather it felt like a holy obligation, a privilege, to give my all to whatever role God was calling me to.

My parents were important role models. They demonstrated a strong work ethic. Both worked outside of our home, while my sister and I were expected to pitch in. Our summers consisted of cleaning the house and helping with my grandparents' vegetable garden. We helped can green beans and tomatoes, freeze corn, shell peas, dig potatoes, and pick strawberries. I still can shuck an ear of corn, clean of all silks in just seconds.

I'm grateful to my parents and grandparents for teaching me the value of hard work. The skills they taught me, along with their common sense, are imbedded in my soul. Their examples are like seeds planted in my heart that have sprouted into mature qualities that have helped me achieve many goals in my professional life and brought me contentment in my personal life.

Latrine duty all those years ago certainly didn't start out as a joyful job, but the way we tackled the task …with fervor and creative flair …brought satisfaction and even today is a strong reminder of important lessons learned.

And, by the way, there was no doubt that we had the best latrine at Camp Cal-Ka-Lin.

TERRI CORNETT

Local Sales Manager, KTUL-TV and First Lady Oklahoma City
Vinita/Tulsa/Oklahoma City, OK

WE MUST FIGHT, FIGHT, FIGHT,
FOR OUR PERSONAL TIME
WITH THE HOLY SPIRIT DAILY
AND EVEN LARGER AMOUNTS
WEEKLY! YES, IT'S IMPORTANT
TO BE CONSCIOUS OF DESTINY
AND OPERATING IN PURPOSE
BUT EVEN MORE IMPORTANT
TO BE DRIVEN FROM THE PLACE
OF INTIMACY WITH GOD.
WHO ARE WE WITHOUT
HIS PERFECT PRESENCE?
LIKE A CAR WITHOUT FUEL...
ALL ABOUT APPEARANCE AND
RUNNING ON OUR OWN FUMES.
WHAT GOOD ARE WE
TO THE WORLD, THEN?
WHAT GOOD ARE WE TO OURSELVES?

TINASHA LA RAYE
Oklahoma City University Graduate

DO NOT LET ANY UNWHOLESOME TALK COME OUT OF YOUR MOUTH,
BUT ONLY WHAT IS HELPFUL FOR BUILDING OTHERS UP
ACCORDING TO THEIR NEEDS, THAT IT MAY BENEFIT THOSE WHO LISTEN.

EPHESIANS 4:29

As I look through a telescope back in time, I see my adult family members using drugs and settling arguments with violence. My mother battled depression and became hooked on prescription medicine as she tried to raise me and my four siblings by herself. Every house we lived in was in shambles and almost always overtaken by roaches. By the age of eight, DHS had removed us from my mother's custody and placed us in my grandparents' home that offered a whole new set of challenges. The house on 3rd Street in Stillwater, Oklahoma, already had seven occupants living there and four of the seven were either addicted to drugs or alcohol. After three years of physical abuse at the hands of one of my uncles, I chose to leave. I spent the next 10 years being shuffled between foster and children's homes. Many of the homes I took refuge in offered some sort of neglect or abuse, but I decided that anything was better than living with my biological family.

In 1988, I became the first person in the history of my family to graduate from high school. After starting a family, I graduated from Oklahoma State University, becoming the first in my family to graduate from college. Today, I am lucky enough to travel all over the U.S. and share my life and book *The Boy Who Carried Bricks* with people of all walks of life. My success and ability to break the cycle came from so many people along the way who had whispered encouragement in my ear. In every school, children's and foster home I lived in, there was at least one person who managed to look past my broken heart and love me no matter how hard I tried to push them away. I can unequivocally say that the reason I am who I am today is because a few dozen people spoke God's truth into my life.

One of the voices of truth came from the soul of a 3rd grade boy during a school assembly I was speaking at. I had finished telling the 300 elementary school students about the challenges I faced during my childhood and was taking questions from the audience. As the students raised their hands to ask questions, the principal would hand the students the microphone so the rest of the audience could hear their question. After I answered 15 or 20 questions, one student asked me where my dad was. I explained that I never got to meet my father because he left before I was born. My answer must have been filled with sadness because as soon as I answered, a 3rd grader from the back of the auditorium raised his hand just before I finished my explanation.

Before the principal could make his way over to the little boy in the back, the boy got up from his seat and walked down to the front of the auditorium where I was standing. Once he was standing beside me, the boy grabbed the mic from me with one hand and reached up and put his other hand on my shoulder. He stood there for a few seconds as I wondered how this would play out. The young boy took a deep breath and said, "Alton, I know you never got a chance to meet your dad, but I want to tell you that I think he missed out."

I was speechless for a moment as tears began to roll down my face. God used that little boy to help me begin to heal a wound that had been haunting me most of my life. This little man also taught me that we should never miss an opportunity to encourage others.

ALTON CARTER

Youth Minister, First United Methodist Church of Stillwater, Author, and Speaker
Stillwater, OK

"HAVE I NOT COMMANDED YOU? BE STRONG AND COURAGEOUS. DO NOT BE AFRAID; DO NOT BE DISCOURAGED, FOR THE LORD YOUR GOD WILL BE WITH YOU WHEREVER YOU GO."

JOSHUA 1:9

It's a cold and windy day in November 1973.

My heart is pounding. After hours of travel, I'm still not ready to leave the plane. We have arrived at Kimpo Airport outside of Seoul, South Korea. My misgivings multiply as I stumble through customs.

For well over a year we have pushed toward this moment, counting on God to direct us on this uncharted path. Why am I suddenly so uneasy and unsure?

Our actions will result in children leaving their homeland; their destinies will be changed forever. Questions flood my mind: Why did we think we could carry out this life-changing responsibility? Who gave us the idea we could or should do this?

Every question brings me closer to full panic. My steps slow to a halt. My husband, Jerry, cheerfully urges me on, seemingly unaware of my hesitations.

Searching the sea of faces, we spot the friendly smile of our newest team member. With an excited wave, Young Kwan guides us outside to the waiting van. I sit in the back listening to the enthusiastic chatter between my husband and Young Kwan. Jerry's voice is confident. I close my eyes and try to pull myself together.

We will be in Seoul for a few days before returning to the States with the first four children. Their adoptive parents are waiting, trusting us to carry out this mission and bring their children home.

After a sleepless night, we meet with Dr. Kim and his staff. Everyone stands when we enter the room. I am embarrassed with such attention and feel unworthy of such a respectful welcome. We are introduced to each person. The names all run together and I am confused even before we begin to look over the paperwork for the children who will be returning with us. All documents are in order and we, with great relief, compliment the good work of the staff. As we leave the office, everyone bows a good-bye.

Then it is time to visit the babies' home a short distance from the office. The soft voices of caretakers and the more demanding cries of the babies surround us. I am paralyzed with emotion. I have never seen this many babies in one room before! How do they manage to attend to each baby?

Mrs. Cho, director of the babies' home, approaches me with one of the infants who will travel with us. I hold my breath as I take her in my arms, expecting her to cry as she looks into my pale, blue-eyed face. She stares at me and I am glued to her sleepy smile. As she puts her head on my shoulder, I realize she has made a holy trust with me.

She is an orphan. She deserves a loving mother and father and a chance to grow, learn, and love. She deserves our very best efforts to pave the way to her future.

Suddenly, the misgivings dissolve. I breathe a prayer of thanksgiving: "Thank you, dear Father, for reminding me that You are in charge. You are directing this endeavor."

I reluctantly return the sleeping baby to her caregiver with a soft kiss and a promise to see her soon for our journey home to her new life.

I wipe tears from my cheeks and turn to look at Jerry. He smiles and nods. My husband knows me well. He has felt my unspoken concerns and questions. He takes my hand and leads me on to the next room crowded with more babies and toddlers. "Come on, Mrs. Dillon. We have work to do. The children are waiting!"

DENIESE DILLON

Co-Founder of Dillon International—Oklahoma's first licensed international adoption agency
Tulsa, OK

NOW FAITH IS CONFIDENCE IN WHAT WE HOPE FOR
AND ASSURANCE ABOUT WHAT WE DO NOT SEE.

HEBREWS 11:1

I can make a difference.

This belief found its way deep into my heart. I never imagined myself trusting God the way I do today. I now have many of my own faith stories to tell, but it wasn't always this way.

Just trust God.

This statement would cause me to envision famous revivalists, like John Wesley and George Whitefield, who impacted thousands. I would think of George Mueller and other spiritual giants only to end up feeling like a grasshopper. I just could not relate.

I can relate now, but I would never have outlined my path to growing in faith the way it happened in my life.

In 1994, I was serving with my family in our inner city church in Des Moines, Iowa. I was home for the summer from Iowa State University and hardly expecting this moment of crisis. I came face-to-face with a situation for which I had neither an answer nor the means to make a difference.

Sasha was 13 years old. She looked sixteen, but she was no more mature than an eight-year-old. Four siblings trailed her like little ducklings as they meandered through the carnival we were hosting in our church parking lot. Something was not right.

In the following weeks, they came to Sunday school, showed up at services, and innocently tested our love for them. The crisis moment came when I finally had the opportunity to solve the big mystery.

On a Wednesday night, I offered to drive them home. We had won their trust and I now was able to carefully ask some questions. Who were their parents? How did they live?

This is what I found.

Dad was a drunk. Mom struggled with drugs and depression. These children lived day in and day out surviving on whatever may or may not be in the refrigerator.

With head hanging down, Sasha explained what life was like inside the walls of this beat-up, two-story place called home. When she finished, we sat in a ten-second moment of silence that seemed like ten minutes. It took everything in me to hold myself together while I said "goodnight" and sent them back into this horror without making a difference for them.

My mind was in anguish with one unreachable thought after another.

I wish I had the money to help them.

I wish I could raise them myself.

I wish I could make a difference!

I found myself crying out to God. This was one of the worst moments of my life.

I said to myself, "When I finish college, I will find a way to make a difference." My prayer was simple, "Use me LORD! I WANT TO MAKE A DIFFERENCE!"

I would love to tell you God spoke to me, but I can't. I would love to have a happy, follow-up story about Sasha, but I don't have one. It took years before I recognized this event as a moment of faith and not failure.

My prayer gave God a blank check to use my life to make a difference. This was an act of faith! From that moment forward, it became much easier to say "Yes" to God. He has not only been faithful, but He has done far beyond what I could ever have imagined.

Apostle Paul says, "faith operates by love." My love for those children activated a greater life of faith. The secret of the spiritual giants is love. Love puts faith to work so we can make a difference like we never imagined.

Be encouraged. Make a difference and just trust God.

CLARENCE HILL, JR

Inaugural Recipient of the SALLT's Clapman Award and
Lead Pastor, Antioch Community Church
Oklahoma City/Norman, OK

LOVE IS PATIENT, LOVE IS KIND. IT DOES NOT ENVY,
IT DOES NOT BOAST, IT IS NOT PROUD.
IT IS NOT RUDE, IT IS NOT SELF-SEEKING, IT IS NOT EASILY ANGERED,
IT KEEPS NO RECORD OF WRONGS...
LOVE NEVER FAILS.

I CORINTHIANS 13:4,8

As I walked into my parents' home, memories rose up to meet me like warmth from an old floor furnace. My glance into the living room caught the lonely piano holding a yellowed page of music. I could almost see my mother in the kitchen, opening the decorated refrigerator door plastered with family pictures. Her old mixer was silent and stood in the corner like a retired soldier no longer called to the duty of stirring up cakes with a beloved grandchild sitting on the cabinet nearby.

My mother no longer rides down the hall in a motorized wheelchair to greet me, but her sweet goodbye lingers forever. Mother had been a fifth grade teacher, and a love lesson was her final gift to me.

It was a day full of changing leaves and cooler winds when I dropped by to see her on my way home from an event in a nearby community. Mother had forgotten I was coming and was asleep. As I leaned over her frail body and kissed her cheek, she opened her eyes. The grogginess of sleep lay over her like a thick veil. She peered straight at me, her 92-year-old brow wrinkled from pain and eyes glazed with slight confusion. "Am I dreaming?" she said.

I laughed and said, "No, I'm here."

In that second she changed. Her eyes focused and brightened, her whole face smiled, and her head made a slight dip as she chuckled. In spite of her years of bad health, she had become more and more loving.

Here was our duet:

"I'm so happy to see you." Her speech had a stroke-induced slur.

"I'm so glad to be here," I replied.

"You're so beautiful." Her eyes seemed to drink me in.

I laughed and returned the compliment.

"I love you so much," she said.

"I love you more." That was always *her* parting comment to everyone.

By now, tears covered my eyes and I pretended it was from the laughter at her outrageous adoration.

She drifted off to sleep again. My schedule was full and I was exhausted. I had planned to stay the night but rationalizing that she would sleep for some time, I went ahead and left. I was busy—wasn't I? Or was the pain of seeing her in such sad shape so uncomfortable that I simply ran away? Now, I wish I had stayed. This is the woman who, while I was in high school, drove me forty-five minutes for private voice lessons after teaching a full day. Once I decided to enter pageants, she was my support system, my chaperone, the one who understood me. She shared my grief when I was left devastated by a divorce and she was the grandmother who helped raise my son. Was I so busy that I couldn't spend that night?

I'm sure she was disappointed when she woke up and I wasn't there. I'm just as sure that she forgave me for leaving. She was like that ...quick to forgive; quicker to love me anyway.

A few weeks after that visit, my husband and I were in Singapore. My sister called with the news that mother had died. I sat down on the sidewalk in tears and whispered a prayer of thanksgiving...for her life, for God's compassion and mercy in taking her with grace, and for that final lovefest between us.

What a blessing to be raised by a parent who heaps unconditional love on her family. We always knew a mother's love; it colors everything.

Because of her, I grew up knowing God's love as well. His love is as much a part of my life as my mother and her mother. It's the *greatest inheritance*. Generation after generation, I've seen the women in my family live the love of

God. They were always the first to rise and the last to retire when caring for their families; always the ones in their churches every Sunday to worship and care for others; always the teachers who made a difference, the ones to write a thoughtful card, call a hurting friend, send some needed food; always the first to forgive.

As I fold the final tender scenes of mother into my heart, I am so grateful that I have experienced this lavish gift of love given to me in order to pass it on: to do good, to help people, to know God. To simply let others know of my love with a look, a smile, a slight chuckle.

Am I dreaming? Or is your face the best gift I could imagine?

JANE JAYROE

Former Miss America, TV News Anchor, Cabinet Secretary of Tourism, Author, Founder, Esther Women, and Oklahoma Hall of Fame Inductee
Sentinel/Laverne/Oklahoma City, OK

FOR THE EYES OF THE LORD SEARCH TO AND FRO
THROUGHOUT THE EARTH THAT HE MIGHT STRONGLY SUPPORT
THOSE HEARTS WHO ARE COMPLETELY HIS.

II CHRONICLES 16:9

It was a Saturday night and I thought the man was pointing at me personally when he, the Reverend Charles Stanley, thrust his bony finger through the TV screen and declared to me, "You can know the purpose of God for your life!"

Well, that was news to me. I was an assistant district attorney at the time, one of fifty serving the Oklahoma County District Attorney's Office. I don't know why it dawned on me that night that God had a plan for my life and that I could know it. I'd been attending church for a long time. You know how we all can hear something said umpteen times then on the umpteenth plus one time we suddenly receive it? Well, this was my umpteenth plus one and the declaration rocked my world.

I spent the next several weeks working through the materials Stanley's folks sent me. They helped me deeply and prayerfully contemplate a number of questions surrounding my passions, skills, and interests together with matters that God seemed to be particularly teaching me. I ended up actually crafting both a vision statement—"Why am I on earth?"—and mission statement— "How do I accomplish the why?" But what was notably odd, I thought, was that here I was a career prosecutor and nothing in either statement said a thing about being a lawyer! Indeed, there were none of the expected buzz phrases associated with my job, which I loved. No "fighting for justice" or "helping crime victims"—nothing. Instead, the phrase that had bubbled up into my mission statement was this: "Helping leaders to stop looking at themselves as leaders who just *happen to be* Christian, but rather as Christian leaders *sent by God* to their spheres of influence, provoking the question, 'So what are you going to do about that?'"

Weird… I had this odd passion to help men and women awaken to God's purposes for their lives as leaders. There was nothing in my background that made a logical connection to that passion so I could only attribute the interest to God's design.

It has now been over fifteen years since that fateful Saturday night. I marvel at God's willingness to aggressively engage in our lives. A few years later, I found myself appointed district attorney in Oklahoma City. I learned what it was like to sit in the hot seat of leadership and to comprehend the challenge of making life and death decisions. I learned what it was like to walk with God in the midst of a maelstrom. I learned to increasingly trust Him even at the embarrassment and humiliation of suffering election defeat. I learned that our heavenly Father is a God of process. That He does not "microwave" us, rather He "marinates" us into becoming the people He requires.

Today, my full-time job is exactly that old mission statement I crafted years ago. He knew I would be doing this all along and prepared me. Today I get the privilege of helping Christian leaders to finish life's course well. But know this, I didn't get a special deal here. My life's experience is purposeful and filled with meaning because that is simply "the deal" God has for all His kids—*if we will pursue Him with all of our heart* (Jeremiah 29:13).

It is a gift He wants each of us to receive.

WES LANE

Former Oklahoma Country District Attorney and Founder, Salt and Light Leadership Training
Oklahoma City, OK

I CAN DO ALL THINGS THROUGH CHRIST WHO STRENGTHENS ME.
PHILIPPIANS 4:13

I came to motherhood late, knowing that a childhood illness had likely left me infertile. So I worked long and hard, was president of my company, and satisfied any maternal instincts I might have denied by being a loving and indulgent aunt. And then one day, God said, "heads up, change is coming." A few months later, God placed my first child into my heart and arms. Today, I have six amazing children that have come into my house in every imaginable way through adoption. Only one of those children was an infant at the time of adoption, the others ranged in age from 3 to 19 years old at the time of their adoption.

The road to adoption is almost never pretty. Substance abuse, mental illnesss, and/or crushing poverty is almost always the catalyst for a biological mother surrendering her child to another. For the adoptive mother, the challenge of unraveling or mitigating the damage while moving forward can be daunting. One particularly difficult night after the adoption of our third child, I cried out, "what was I thinking, why am I doing this? My life was just fine a few years ago and now I am constantly exhausted, confused, and frustrated." Out of the darkness, the answer came. "Because you can." Philippians 4:13 teaches us that "I can do all things through Christ who strengthens me." God was reminding me that he had blessed me repeatedly and now, armed with the strength of our Lord, He had made me ready for the challenge.

Over and over again, God, through my children, has taught me lessons. One of the most important came from my fifth child. This child came to me from a home filled with violence, rage, and sexual and physical abuse, so God had to really step in and guide.

This child could lie to me about the color of the sky when we both were looking at it. He had learned to lie at an early age to escape a beating or to avoid being locked in a closet for days and he saw no reason to stop. I tried taking his phone away for a day, a week, several weeks, a month, and finally a year, each time telling him that trust was central to our family and I couldn't trust him. As that year was drawing to a close, I realized I had no place left to go; I certainly wasn't going to beat him, even though he expected it, and I certainly wasn't going to give up, even though he wanted it. One day as I was nearing the breaking point, God spoke and said, "hold on Missy [sometimes God sounds like my mother], this isn't about you trusting him; this is about him trusting you."

I went back to my child and asked what I could do to help him trust that I was always going to act in his best interest. He thought about it a few days and came back with a proposal that he and I should talk every day, about big or little things, it didn't matter; just that we talked every day. And in those daily talks, our relationship began to blossom and trust took root. I won't tell you that this beautiful child never lies to me now; but I can tell you that it is rare enough that I am always surprised. What God revealed to me about trust and my child is applicable to our trust in God. Every day He asks of us, "what is it going to take for you to trust that I am going to act in your best interest." And the answer is as simple as the one my son landed on, developing a relationship by talking to God every day. Through my children, I have learned that trust is built and deepened in that daily conversation with God.

NATALIE SHIRLEY

President & CEO, National Cowboy and Western Heritage Museum,
Former Oklahoma Secretary of Commerce and Tourism,
President of OSU/OKC,
Oklahoma Secretary for Education & Workforce Development, and
President of ICIM Insurance Group
Blackwell/Oklahoma City, OK

LIKE ANY FRIENDSHIP, YOU MUST WORK AT DEVELOPING YOUR FRIENDSHIP WITH GOD. IT WON'T HAPPEN BY ACCIDENT. IT TAKES DESIRE, TIME AND ENERGY.

RICK WARREN
The Purpose Driven Life

WHAT TIME I AM AFRAID, I WILL TRUST IN THEE.
PSALMS 56:3

My doctor didn't mince words.

"Shannon, I've discovered a cyst on your left ovary."

Pow.

My life changed in the blink of an eye.

In my gymnastics career I'd taken many hard falls and suffered numerous painful injuries, but never had I felt such seismic shock to my body as when I heard my doctor's words.

I just thank God I heard them. It's by the grace of God that I was there. I had almost postponed my appointment. Because of my demanding schedule, I'd called my doctor to reschedule this appointment. But, I was put on hold. And in those few seconds, I felt a tinge of guilt for not practicing what I preached to others about taking care of your health. I could swear I heard from above a whispering in my ear, "Don't delay!" So instead of postponing the appointment, I took the first one. Within an hour, my life had changed forever.

Weeks later, an ultrasound showed a large mass on my left ovary. Surgery followed and then confirmation.

I had ovarian cancer. A terribly serious diagnosis.

I felt that my body had betrayed me. It had served me so well in all those years of competition.

I started in gymnastics at the age of five in Edmond, Oklahoma. By the age of 15, I was blessed to be a member of the 1992 Olympic team in Barcelona and then in 1996 I was on the "Magnificent Seven" team at the Olympics in Atlanta. People remember me as the spitfire from Oklahoma with the frizzy hair and the trademark scrunchie. By the age of nineteen, I had become the most decorated gymnast, male or female, in U.S. History. I wouldn't trade a second of my young life that was full of competing and traveling. My family kept me grounded and my teachers at school allowed me to have a somewhat normal life for a shy teenager who was gone a lot.

But life didn't end after my career as a gymnast. It was a huge adjustment with some big challenges, but over time I found my way. After graduating from college and law school I began to establish my new career.

Life had finally settled into a wonderful pattern of purpose and contentment. I moved to Florida and married the most amazing man. I had started my business, Shannon Miller Lifestyle, a company dedicated to empowering women to make their health a priority. And we were blessed with a baby boy, Rocco. Life couldn't have been better!

Then cancer happened—shocking and unexpected—just like it is for the millions of other people it attacks every day. Having Olympic medals didn't count for a thing when facing this dreaded disease, but my tough training did. I knew how to set goals, eliminate negative thoughts, accept help from others, and keep moving forward one small step at a time. I prepared for battle.

Throughout my life of competition, my mom had always tucked note cards with scriptures in my travel bag. That served as great reminders of God's faithfulness in my life and my mother's deep love. My family gave me that kind of spiritual foundation growing up. It was my rock as an adult. I still had those note cards during the nine weeks of grueling chemotherapy and I would reread my mother's special messages.

I am a planner and a perfectionist by nature, but I found early on that while it's admirable to shoot for perfection, it's not about perfect. It's about going out and giving it your best every single day. It's about getting back up after you've been knocked down. Cancer is a formidable opponent but I was determined not to be a victim, no matter what the outcome. Setting goals and working hard to achieve them was one way I could have some control. Some days my goal was just to get out of bed and get dressed.

Today, I am cancer free, and the mother of another child, our daughter, Sterling. Recently, I wrote a book about my life's journey, *It's Not About Perfect.* I wanted to share my gymnastics journey and encourage other people who are facing cancer or any other challenge in their life.

My hair has grown back, my children are growing up, my business and foundation work continues to expand, my marriage is blessed.

I thank God every day for life. And while scars from the illness may remain, to me they simply serve as reminders to live life to the fullest each and every day.

SHANNON MILLER

Olympic Gymnast, Author, Motivational Speaker, Founder, Shannon Miller Lifestyle, and Oklahoma Hall of Fame Inductee
Edmond, OK/Jacksonville, FL

DO UNTO OTHERS AS YOU WOULD HAVE THEM DO UNTO YOU.

LUKE 6:30

My dad enjoyed a lot about life, but he was most passionate about building a company where employees could grow and succeed. He was always driven to "do the right thing." I guess you could say Chester Cadieux tried to live by the golden rule, "Do unto others as you would have them do unto you." It sounds simple; just treat people the way you want to be treated. But then, my dad was simple like that—down to earth—but smart. That combination and a lot of hard work built a heck of a company.

In 1958, Chester Cadieux II, and business partner Burt B. Homes, founded QuikTrip in Tulsa with $16,000 in initial capital. The company has steadily grown into an $11-billion company with more than 700 stores, 19,700 employees, and its own distribution network across an 11-state footprint. And we're still growing.

I've been blessed to be a part of this company for more than twenty-five years. I started working on the front lines of QuikTrip as a part-time clerk when I was 16 years old. After graduating from The University of Tulsa with a degree in management, I went to work on the graveyard shift in the stores. It was quite a lifestyle change from sweet college life to working six nights a week.

Dad taught me a lot about the business, but he also taught me about the importance of service within the community. He spent a lot of time volunteering in community leadership positions. There was one area of leadership that he felt particularly strong about—the education of Christian ministers. His mother, my grandmother, was a big influence on our family. Her faith was strong and her love for the church was an important part of family life. Dad used to say that his standard for success was simple: at the end of the day would he be proud to tell his mom what he had done that day? I'm sure his mother would have been very proud of the fact that dad not only provided resources but leadership to the Phillips Theological Seminary for many years. Dad felt that a solid education was critical to the future of the church. He believed that the church and its leaders were important to individuals, but also to society as a whole. "The world needs good pastors," he would often say.

I have tried to follow in my dad's footsteps in my community volunteer efforts and growing the company. The culture he created at QuikTrip continues today as a place of opportunity and fairness. As I look out from our business offices and know the incredible employees I get to interact with every day, I know that God has blessed a lot of folks through my dad's productive life. Much of his work ethic was a result of what he believed was his responsibility to God.

The legacy of QuikTrip is important for what it provides for others. But nothing is more significant than the standards Dad left within his own family of valuing other people ...as you would even yourself.

CHET CADIEUX III

CEO, QuikTrip Corporation
Tulsa, OK

THEREFORE EVERYONE WHO HEARS THESE WORDS OF MINE
AND PUTS THEM INTO PRACTICE IS LIKE A WISE MAN
WHO BUILT HIS HOUSE ON THE ROCK.
THE RAIN CAME DOWN, THE STREAMS ROSE AND
THE WINDS BLEW AND BEAT AGAINST THAT HOUSE;
YET IT DID NOT FALL,
BECAUSE IT HAD ITS FOUNDATION ON THE ROCK.

MATTHEW 7:24-25

The rains and winds came to my life unexpectedly some years ago and I thought I was going to drown at times.

Nothing prepared me for the tragic news following the joyful birth of my daughter, Heather, in 1993. Life had always been an expected upward path for me. I was raised in a great family, full of love and optimism. My mom was constantly creating special moments in life, even when I didn't recognize them. She also focused on pointing out the importance of planning my future. Her influence led me into a challenging and rewarding career as a petroleum engineer leading to a job with Kerr-McGee in Louisiana.

My beloved wife of two years and I jumped into life there, learning to love everything Cajun. We started building our first new home—all 1,700 square feet of it. Even better than that, we were expecting our first baby. When the birth happened, there were a few complications but everything seemed fine. But in a few weeks, my wife began having headaches that went from bad to worse. Early one Sunday, while I was out working before church, my wife called. She said her headache was really bad and it wouldn't go away. Soon, we heard the dreaded diagnosis of brain cancer. We began a two-year journey of brain surgery, chemotherapy, and all the possible things to imagine and try. Then, drowning in my own grief, I had to explain to a three-year-old little girl that her mommy had gone to heaven.

After the funeral, when all the family and friends had left, it was the two of us. I knew I had to get past the loss and into a life for this child. The question I kept asking myself was "How can I be the best dad? How can I provide for the future she needs?" I knew I couldn't do it. So on my knees, my prayer was that God would sustain me. My prayer was that He would help me do the best for her, for Heather.

My foundation of faith held me up. It was my rock.

I wanted Heather to remember her childhood with fondness like I did. I remembered how my parents were. I remembered their love and hope for a better future for me. What was my daughter going to remember? A mad dad, a stressed dad, fear, frustration? Or was she going to remember happiness?

With that mindset, I determined to be strong and make the most of my time with Heather, even after long days at the office.

There were so many challenges—big and small. I struggled with how to create a pseudo resemblance that our home wasn't just a man's place. I got into the habit of buying fresh flowers every week. So many times I'd walk by those flowers and say, "That's $9 or that's $10 and they'll die in three days." But I found that small efforts were important in creating a home for us. I couldn't be mother and dad, but I could try to make moments special.

Fortunately, I didn't have to do it alone. God provided so much support for me—family, friends, my church, my company, and my community. That kind of help is critical to any single parent.

I have been so blessed since that time, personally and professionally. Today, that little girl makes her daddy proud every day as a young adult woman. We have both been blessed with my remarriage to a wonderful person and the birth of triplets, then a son, and now another daughter. I am the business leader of one of the finest companies in America where we are deeply involved in creating a better community.

Every day I am grateful for the support I've had along the way and the blessings of each moment. I don't claim to be the "wise" man in the scripture who knows to build his house foundation on the rock of faith, but I do know what holds firm when the winds and rain come in life …a loving and merciful God.

DOUG LAWLER

CEO, Chesapeake Energy Corp.
Oklahoma City, OK

PEACE I LEAVE WITH YOU; MY PEACE I GIVE YOU.
I DO NOT GIVE TO YOU AS THE WORLD GIVES.
DO NOT LET YOUR HEARTS BE TROUBLED AND DO NOT BE AFRAID.

JOHN 14:27

One of the happiest moments of my life came from a simple, spontaneous, time with my family. My husband and I were driving back home from Texas with our three young children in the back seat. We crossed the Red River and saw the sign that welcomed us to "Oklahoma." All three kids in the back seat started yelling and singing the song, "Oklahoma!," and sang it all the way to the end. We were home—Oklahoma. I had tears in my eyes; they had no idea what a long life journey it was to get *home*.

When I was two years old and living in El Salvador, my father divorced my mother and left us—four children with a now single mother in a war torn country. She did the best thing she could do for us, she put us with family and went to America. There, she worked two or three jobs, saving as much as possible to try and get her children to this land of opportunity. It took four years but when I was six years old, we came to America. My mother's faith never faltered. She trusted the Lord every step of the way. I never saw her weaken. She believed with her whole heart that if we kept God at the front of our lives, and worked hard, we would do well in America. Her other lesson was that we must always give back.

We learned the English language in a matter of months, playing in the neighborhoods of New Jersey and attending good schools. While other kids grew up wanting a car, I wanted only one thing: to become a U.S. citizen. I felt like an American, I believed I was a part of this country but it wasn't until I had the paper in hand, that I really knew I belonged to this great Nation. It's a blessing as an adult today to help others in this process and to also stress the importance of getting involved in community and engaged as an informed voter. You can be a citizen by choice or by birth. But, either way, we must never take it for granted.

After becoming a citizen and earning an Associates degree, I moved to Texas to finish my Bachelor's degree. There I met my husband, Ezequiel Hernandez, whose family originated from Mexico.

We married and were settled in Texas when an opportunity came along in Oklahoma City. After much prayer we both felt that God was calling us to Oklahoma—not just to open a business, but also to settle in this place. Once the decision was made, we both had such peace about the move. It truly was the peace that passes all understanding. We knew in our hearts that this was the soil where God wanted to plant our lives. This is where we wanted to have our children.

In 2002, we moved to Oklahoma City. The people have been so welcoming and are so genuine. Maybe it's the resilience of the people, maybe Oklahoma's history reminds me of the hardiness of my mother's journey, maybe it's the great opportunities that abound here, but there's a spirit in Oklahoma that blesses me and grows our family in all the important ways …including our spiritual lives.

My mom sacrificed so much so I could take advantage of opportunities I would not have had in El Salvador. Her faith in God and her work ethic have made my current life possible. Every day I am thankful and I pray that I will always try to encourage and empower others so they, too, can grow in God's grace and benefit from the opportunities of America.

ESTELLA HERNANDEZ

Realtor, Keller Williams, and Community Volunteer
El Salvador/Oklahoma City, OK

WE DON'T SEE THINGS CLEARLY. WE'RE SQUINTING IN A FOG, PEERING THROUGH A MIST. BUT IT WON'T BE LONG BEFORE THE WEATHER CLEARS AND THE SUN SHINES BRIGHT!

1 CORINTHIANS 13:12

IRREVERSIBLE COMA—Those two horrible words from the concerned brain surgeon shook the foundation of the Burke family. The doctor spoke softly as he described the finality of the damage that had struck the brain stem of an otherwise healthy and robust 35-year-old missionary, Robert Burke, known to his parishioners in the inner city of Oklahoma City as Pastor Rob.

Pastor Rob was my first-born son. As a young adult he learned that my oft-repeated phrase, "Life is a Series of Choices," was unequivocally true. He chose to become a musician, then chose law school, but something tugged at his heart that put him at a crossroads in his life. He and his new wife, Deborah, felt God calling them to full-time ministry. He completely understood that leaving law school to become a youth pastor could greatly impede his financial progress. But, he made the right choice, and entered the ministry.

In a blur of a few years, Pastor Rob founded Inner City Church, a risky effort to reach adults and children in Oklahoma City's poorest neighborhoods. Despite failed programs that had come before him, he made a choice. He would obey God! On Father's Day 2003, the church opened with 30 people present. Three years later, a variety of programs from free haircuts, student mentoring, and free Sunday dinner brought 400 people his way each week.

He was at a crossroads again. Would his church have the same music and same approach as other churches? Pastor Rob knew that even though the message of salvation had not changed, it was necessary to change the way in which the message was presented. In 2006, when Hobby Lobby founder David Green offered to donate a 70,000-square-foot former church complex in south Oklahoma City to him, Rob had to choose from being comfortable with his successful mission, or launch a larger and more complex missionary effort. As expected, he chose the latter and completely trusted God to make it all happen.

Life was good. Pastor Rob loved his parishioners and was an exceptional husband to his wife, Deborah, and father to his young sons, Nathan and Jon. Then, Pastor Rob began having headaches on a frequent basis. When the headaches became so severe that he was throwing up, Deborah insisted he seek medical attention. Doctors found a tumor that occupied nearly one-fourth of his brain. Within a few days, a brain surgeon removed the tumor. For the first 36 hours, Rob did not need pain medication and had one of the best, pain-free days in months.

On Sunday morning, two days after the first surgery, Rob developed a headache. He was given heavy medicine and simply never woke up again. During the hours after the surgery, his brain swelled and damaged his brain steam beyond repair.

Pastor Rob had made the right choices for himself in his young life. Now, the family was left with choices. After much prayer, we decided to terminate life support, thanking God that at least Rob was spared a long and painful illness and death

After the shock of Rob's death, I had to make a choice. Would I let my son's death haunt the rest of my life and ruin my relationship with everyone around me? I knew I had a reason to withdraw—losing a child is one of the most devastating events in life. I also knew that I was the only grandfather for my seven- and five-year-old grandsons. My prayer was simple, "God, I can make it through this horrific grief only with your help. Please let something good come out of this tragedy. Help me make the right choices that will honor You and Rob's work."

Eight years later, God has been faithful. Deborah made the choice to continue the Inner City Church she and Rob founded. With a team of volunteers, they moved into the expansive old church complex and have multiplied many times over the assistance given the people that Rob loved so much. For me, God has blessed me abundantly by giving me the opportunity to influence Nathan and Jon in their walk with Christ. Now teenagers, both are faithful Christians and a tribute to their father's and mother's training.

Life will always be a series of choices. But, if we choose correctly, God will help us through any season of trouble. As Pastor Rob often said to his congregation, "Nothing is impossible with God!"

BOB BURKE

Attorney, Author, Historian, and Oklahoma Hall of Fame Inductee
Broken Bow/Oklahoma City, OK

BLESSED IS THE NATION WHOSE GOD IS THE LORD

PSALMS 33:12

I grew up outside of Dale, Oklahoma, in Pottawatomie County, population 181. We didn't have much in material things but I had the best of families. Little did I know during those early years, but God planted the seed to my military career through the passion of my father.

Rhoper Bly, my dad, always felt a special calling to serve America. He wanted to join the military, but was turned down because of a heart murmur. He was classified 4F. He was devastated. He rebounded, as he always did, and went to work for the Air Force at Tinker Air Force Base as a civilian. He started at the very bottom of the classification pole, but rose through the jobs because of his tenacity, curiosity, and dedication to be the best he could be.

I never thought much about that influence until I found myself in a crises situation. I was a schoolteacher and single mother of two small girls. I worked additional jobs to hold my little family together. Teachers were going to strike in 1979 and I knew I couldn't go without my salary. But I didn't want to disappoint my colleagues and cross the line so I had to make a really tough decision. A friend at church suggested I join the Air National Guard. I didn't hesitate. They sent me to Basic Air Force Training and that changed my life forever.

God had his hand on my little girls and me. My mother stepped in to keep the girls when I attended training. I found out very quickly that I was destined to serve my country and my community.

For 22 years I continued to train and serve in the Air National Guard and teach school. I became a principal and had a wonderful chance to touch the lives of children, parents, and teachers. I stressed patriotism, individual accountability, achievement, and others before self. The Air Force Core Values were applicable to us all.

All the while, God was preparing me for a higher calling and more responsibility. As a woman, I was given the first unit to Command in the state of Oklahoma. It was a real test. Airmen, older than me, having much more time in the Air Guard than I, tested my determination and heart to lead. I wanted to succeed because being the "first" meant so many other women depended on my success for their future opportunities. It meant even more in the big picture, I was preparing airmen for the tests of their life in battle. Being a leader was more than just knowledge, it meant having the heart to recognize their struggles and help them find solutions to difficulties that could be life threatening. I served four more command positions after that, each of them larger than the previous.

I was given the opportunity to go active duty to serve the state under the Adjutant General (Commander of Army and Air in the state of Oklahoma). So, I retired from my education position and wore the uniform all the time. My children were grown, I was blessed with a husband who worked hard and supported my being engaged with my mission for long hours, days, and sometimes weeks.

In 2003, I become the first woman general officer in the Oklahoma Air Guard and the first woman of Native American ancestry to become a General in the nation. I believe that I was trained from a small child to serve, to learn, to put others first, and to be the best I could be. I found that the "brotherhood" of general officers felt the weight of leadership as I did. Most all of them were deeply spiritual people. It was very supportive to be able to discuss serious life threatening situations and pray with my contemporaries about God's direction and wisdom to lead.

I am just an ordinary woman who loves God and His people. I volunteered for a life that turned out to be more than anticipated. By putting faith in Him, I helped my children, touched thousands, and did what I could to protect this one Nation under God.

MAJOR GENERAL (RET.) RITA ARAGON
Air National Guard, Oklahoma Secretary of Military and Veterans Affairs,
and Oklahoma Hall of Fame Inductee
Dale/Edmond, OK

I MAY NOT KNOW
WHAT MY FUTURE HOLDS,
BUT I DO KNOW
WHO
HOLDS THAT FUTURE,
SO MY GOAL IN LIFE
IS TO STAY NEAR
THE GUIDE.

REV. WAYNE CORDEIRO
The Divine Mentor

FOR TRULY, I SAY TO YOU, IF YOU HAVE FAITH
LIKE A GRAIN OF MUSTARD SEED, YOU WILL SAY TO THIS MOUNTAIN,
'MOVE FROM HERE TO THERE,' AND IT WILL MOVE,
AND NOTHING WILL BE IMPOSSIBLE FOR YOU.

MATTHEW 17:20

Police and ambulance lights rotated all around me as I drove up on the scene of the accident. My son, Brandon, had been on a motorcycle that ran into a brick mailbox at 60 miles per hour.

When I got to the hospital, they told me he'd passed away. I got to hold him that last time. There are no words to describe the feeling. How could this have happened to Brandon? But it did, and all because some guy said "Take one of these" years earlier and Brandon didn't know that he wouldn't be able to stop.

Of five children and stepchildren, Brandon had been the easiest to raise and the one who caused the least trouble. It never occurred to me that my perfect son, the handsome college football star, might be addicted to drugs. Then one night, while driving his girlfriend home, Brandon lost control of the car. The vehicle flipped, plunging the couple into a creek, where they dangled upside down for what seemed like hours. Lying in a hospital bed, his body battered and broken, Brandon admitted, "I was drinking, and I took prescription drugs."

Brandon healed from his injuries, but his beloved girlfriend didn't. Her death was something from which he never recovered.

For the next two years, he struggled to break free from his addiction.

I admitted him to a rehabilitation center, and that worked for a while, but eventually he began using drugs again. Willpower wasn't enough.

The death of my son seemed to end my own life. Yet, I had to pull myself together, because I had other kids. Days were hard but I had work; I didn't know how I was going to make it through the nights. It was a nightmare.

My depression lingered, but a couple of good friends were determined not to let me wallow too long in my grief. They insisted I go to Africa with them. Finally, I agreed to the trip.

When I got to Uganda, I met Sister Rosemary Nyirumbe. I was fascinated with this diminutive nun who openly defied guerilla leader Joseph Kony and the Lord's Resistance Army and saved hundreds of lives from civil war by providing sanctuary at her convent's practical training center. I wanted to help with her life-changing work. We formed an organization called Pros for Africa and have been supporting Sister Rosemary's work since 2003.

That trip helped me get my focus off myself and on to others in need. It saved my life. I began to see other ways I could help myself through the loss of Brandon.

My teenage daughter told me she had a friend that had a real struggle with drugs. She asked me if I would talk to him. I did. He was the first kid I ever talked to and shared Brandon's story. You know what? This kid turned his life around.

So, I began to talk to various people and tell them the story. Then I talked to schools and ultimately colleges. By now, I've lost count how many times I've told this story.

I think of the word "fate" a lot. I don't think anybody's fate is cast in stone forever. I think that there is hope. That's why we started an organization called FATE, Fighting Addiction Through Education. The purpose of that organization is to tell stories like Brandon's, and there are so many. But we also share the stories of others who make it.

Brandon would be proud of what we're doing. He would be proud of me that I just didn't die.

The death of a child leaves a deep wound that never completely goes away, no matter how much time passes. But I began to feel better. Sharing my time, energy, and resources with those less fortunate—something I'd never thought much about—was like balm for the soul, a sort of spiritual medicine that soothed the ache over losing my boy.

By helping someone else, my life made more sense.

REGGIE WHITTEN

Attorney, Author, Founder, Pros For Africa and FATE,
and Oklahoma Hall of Fame Inductee
Seminole/Oklahoma City, OK

THEY WILL FIGHT AGAINST YOU BUT WILL NOT OVERCOME YOU,
FOR I AM WITH YOU AND WILL RESCUE YOU.

JEREMIAH 1:19

I will be the first to admit that every Sunday I am not in a pew in my house of worship. Some of my deepest interactions with Him have been on our front porch in the country, reading scripture or devotionals, and looking over the vast landscape He has created and populated. It is intimate. It is fulfilling. It is magical. It is with Him that I have my first conversation each morning and the last conversation each night.

My greatest blessing is the fact that He had a plan for me from the very beginning. I also believe that blessings can be as painful as they can be joyous. "Blessed Beyond Measure" is my mantra.

I have been blessed with the most amazing parents, a large extended family, and a loyal and supportive husband, who just happened to be my junior high sweetheart. My dream of being a mother came true with the birth of my son. And, years later, a second joined our family. Those sweet boys have given me two sweet girls—marrying on the same weekend two years apart.

Friendships also have been an enormous blessing in my life, the longest and most significant my best friend since sixth grade—Scharlotte. It is through her journey that I have leaned on Him the most, praised Him the most, and, yes, even tested Him the most. It is through her that I was reminded again and again that He has us in His hands.

In April, 2011, while Scharlotte underwent a biopsy, her husband mentioned an offer he had received from his employer for a local position— no more traveling. Little did we know then how important that offer would be. God was putting everything in place for the battle that lie ahead.

Metastatic, triple negative breast cancer—the most treatment-resistant breast cancer already had moved to her lymph nodes. An aggressive chemotherapy regimen, double mastectomy, more chemotherapy, radiation, and reconstruction followed. She checked appointments, treatments, and procedures off her list with strength and grace for the better part of the next three years.

On her last day of radiation, she walked out of the doctor's office physically and emotionally empty. She made it clear that was her *last* treatment, regardless of what the future held. I was so angry—angry with her for deciding no more treatment even if it was needed and angry with Him for allowing her to be in this place. Less than two weeks later we learned the cancer was gone. I remember thanking Him for healing her cancer, giving her the strength to endure the many treatments and surgeries, and for making her whole again. I also asked for forgiveness for my anger.

Next, the focus turned to recurrence. The goal was to hit the five-year mark when the percentage of the cancer's return dropped to 1-3%. The following months and years we vacationed, we celebrated, and did things that previously had been of no interest to her. My daily prayers always included my gratitude for healing her.

We made it—five years! The immediate panic of every twinge, cramp, or bump being cancer was replaced with a sense of euphoria. And then, within months, what we thought was a virus was the side effect of the breast cancer returning in her brain. My daily prayers became mixed with gratefulness for the time given and anger for the cruelty.

After two brain surgeries and more radiation, her doctor said, "For every one tumor we see [there were five], there are three or four we can't see." In that moment I saw in her both devastation and relief.

The next few weeks included doctor's appointments, hospital stays, and very little real "Scharlotte" time—she was there, but not really there. On the night we brought her home for the last time, He gave us an incredible gift—lucidity and clarity. That night I became her scribe as she reeled off her instructions and wishes. She also said, "I knew the day of the biopsy I would never beat this."

Her last night with us, I prayed for Him to take her, to stop the pain. I prayed for that chance of a miracle. And, the selfish part of me, prayed to Him not to take my best friend. He understood. Home with Him and whole again, she was finally cured.

Throughout this journey I never once questioned my faith, but I did test it. My prayers were not always of gratitude. But He just kept providing, unwavering in His love. I have often wondered why the battle was so long if her fate had been determined. What I know now is that He was answering *her* prayers for the strength and wisdom to fight for all of us, because that is what *we* needed. Truly, "Blessed Beyond Measure."

GINI MOORE CAMPBELL

Editor, Author, Scriptwriter,
and Vice President, Oklahoma Hall of Fame and Gaylord-Pickens Museum
Oklahoma City, OK

HE WHO HATH EARS TO HEAR; LET HIM HEAR.

MATTHEW 13:9

For years I had heard of the extraordinary work of Dr. Jack Hough in Oklahoma City but I never dreamed he would have such an impact on the direction of my life. At the time of our meeting, I was serving in the Army as an ear nose and throat surgeon.

Jack and I shared so many interests: We both understood that all of life is sacred and there are no divisions between what we believe at church and how we live at work. It's all about God, through God, and by God.

Our first project together was a mission trip to Russia for almost four weeks. We went to three different locations putting on medical conferences and sharing the gospel. Following this time, Jack invited me to join him in Oklahoma City when my time with the Army was completed.

In 2004, we all moved to Oklahoma City, my wife and three children. Unfortunately, Dr. Hough died in 2012, but his vision continues.

Our work at the Hough Ear Institute is not just about physical needs, but also spiritual needs. When we read the scripture about "ears that hear" we understand that people need to hear physically, but it's also important to hear spiritually. The woman at the well was thirsty for physical water but received living water and her testimony moved an entire village to follow Jesus (John 4:1-42).

We believe that if we pay attention to this mission that God will multiply our efforts. There are several ways that is happening: We have a fellowship program for foreign doctors. When they come here to study at the Hough Ear Institute, they live in our homes. They participate in our lives, which include church and Bible Study. One example is a doctor from southeast Asia who became a Christian and led his whole family to Jesus. An excellent ear surgeon, he travels all over the region near his home, spreading the *Good News*.

Another effort is our research laboratory. Dr. Hough was always looking for ways to make things better. Our goal is to *restore hearing through medication*. It's a God-size project. Many researchers are from other countries. A lot of them become believers and influence their families, neighborhoods, and countries.

Another way God multiplies our efforts is when we offer our own work. Four years ago, my wife and I were preparing to go to a city in the Middle East to see our new grandchild. Before we left, I saw myself in a dream working in a tent, doing an ear clinic in Lebanon. When I woke up, I thought to myself, "No, we're going to see our new baby, not work." But God is persuasive and opened the door for us to serve in a Syrian refugee camp. God gave me specific words and encouragement from Isaiah 29:18 "And in that day shall the deaf hear the words of the book and the blind will see through the gloom and darkness." These are words God gave us and He is always faithful.

What happened there was miraculous, but in ways we couldn't have imagined. We had two tents to serve the patients in the Syrian refugee camp. One was an ear clinic and the other was a pharmacy and a place to pray. That tent was loaned to us by one of the women there. Over time, she became an amazing Jesus Follower who now leads a group of 12 women who lead a group of about 250 women, mostly widows. That initial clinic has been multiplied into 16 different clinics in 16 different refugee camps. One can see how the truth of Isaiah 60:22 works out in God's hands: "The smallest family will become a thousand people, and the tiniest group will become a mighty nation. At the right time, I, the LORD, will make it happen." Our team in the Middle East continues to check on progress and offer support. There have been confirmed reports of healings …lame who walk, blind who see, and deaf who hear.

We know that miracles occur. The ordinary process of hearing is miraculous. And seeing hearing restored is a Holy moment. Witnessing a baby hear the voice of their mother for the first time is one of the great joys of our profession.

Dr. Jack Hough always encouraged others to see miracles in this way ...whether it's an unexplained instantaneous healing or a medical healing performed with surgery and/or modern medicine ...*all healing is from God; it's all miracle!*

RICHARD KOPKE, MD, FACS

CEO, Hough Ear Institute, Affiliated with: Otologic Medical Clinic
Integris Medical Center
Oklahoma City, OK

AND WE KNOW THAT ALL THINGS WORK TOGETHER FOR GOOD TO THEM THAT LOVE GOD, TO THEM WHO ARE THE CALLED ACCORDING TO HIS PURPOSE.

ROMANS 8:28

When I was three years old, doctors told my mother, Queenie, that I had spinal meningitis and wasn't going to live. My mother listened, then went to the great physician, Jesus, and begged for my life. The next day, when the doctors were amazed to see me doing better, they told mother that if I survived, I would be mentally retarded and physically disabled.

With a slight smile, Queenie said, "Uh-huh." She knew God had answered her prayer and the death sentence was repealed.

In the inner city, life was not easy for us. My parents divorced when I was six. Mom cleaned other people's houses. She was my heart and strength with an unshakable faith in God. She raised us up in a rich Christian heritage amid the chaos of the housing complex.

My life changed when President John F. Kennedy instituted the National Physical Fitness Program, which required all high school students to have their fitness level compared to students in other countries. This test brought some very high points for me. The physical education teacher encouraged me to come out for girls' sports. I participated in three sports; we were winners in all three.

Our team needed someone to run the 440 dash in track. At five feet, nine inches, I was the logical one. Once I got out there I realized that behind my shy introverted exterior, lurked a tiger. More importantly, I recognized with each year and each track experience that *I was made to run*. It was definitely part of God's plan for me.

Track led to a scholarship to college. Training hard, running fast, the sport led to international travel, four Olympic teams, and Gold and Silver Olympic medals. I was the first and only woman to win Gold in the 800-meter run. I held that record for fifteen years, as well as other Olympic and world records for track.

At the Summer Olympics of 1976, in Montreal, I was favored to win the women's 800-meter race. But something went very wrong.

In my semifinal race, the unthinkable happened: I ran a very lethargic race and couldn't break out of myself, no matter how hard I tried. My body just refused to obey instructions. I seemed to be stuck on slow-motion autopilot. Confused, stunned, fearful, and in disbelief, I walked off the track—last.

Leaving the Games, depressed, I received an invitation to run one more time in a U.S. versus U.S.S.R. meet in Maryland before returning home. I only said "yes" because they had offered a stipend big enough to cover my rent.

I approached the line not caring about the outcome, until a teammate of mine hollered out words of encouragement from the stands. It was like being reminded of the purpose for which I had been born: "Run for Jesus!"

I felt adrenaline pumping through my body as it prepared to run its normal elite level. I prayed a quick prayer, "Okay, Father, this one's for You. It's my tribute run to Jesus." My nerves shot off like Fourth of July fireworks as I stepped to the line, fired up to run the race of my life.

I finished simultaneously with a Russian runner—a personal best for both of us and a new American record for me. By honoring God in the presence of witnesses, my tribute run worked out to my good.

Even when we don't understand what God is doing in the moment, *He always knows what He is achieving for the long run.* He's more interested in our character than our comfort.

Since then, my race has taken different paths. I have been a Gospel singer-songwriter, speaker, author, and ordained minister. For twenty-five years I served in the Olympic chaplaincy program and completed a Masters of Divinity and ultimately a Doctorate of Ministry in Sports Chaplaincy. I am *still* running for Jesus.

MADELINE MANNING MIMS

Olympic Athlete, Speaker, Singer, Author, and Chaplain
Tulsa, OK

I CAN DO ALL THINGS THROUGH CHRIST WHO STRENGTHENS ME.

PHILIPPIANS 4:13

How many times have I come back to this verse over my 38 years in the broadcast industry...too many to count. Just like your job, TV news can be a very tough business. TV news can drain you—physically, emotionally, and spiritually. Whether it's carrying 50 pounds of camera equipment through 102-degree Oklahoma heat, sitting just a few feet away from a grieving mother giving a tearful news conference pleading with anyone to help find her child's killer, or anchoring hours of continuous live coverage of a killer tornado and seeing the devastation and shock and despair of fellow Oklahomans, there's so much tragedy you have to rub shoulders with every day.

But it's also an incredible blessing. You get to help people like I just mentioned with their problems. You get to spread the word through the far-reaching power of TV to help that grieving mother and those victims of our violent weather. And no other people respond to the aid of their neighbors like Oklahomans. And, of course, there's the other side of TV news. You get to come face to face with fascinating people from around the world—presidents, celebrities, and real heroes of our military and police or fire departments. There's no other job like it! And you better be good at it or you won't last long in this business. And if there's one thing I've learned over all these years... I'm not good enough.

I don't have the news gravitas of a Jack Ogle, or the TV personality of Linda Cavanaugh, or the poise of a Jane Jayroe. For me to be able sit on the Channel 4 set at 6:00 p.m. and 10:00 p.m. and deliver the news to tens of thousands of people successfully every night, I need help. LOTS. OF. HELP.

"I can do all things through Christ who strengthens me"—has become my prayer, in one form or another, every day before work. Without Christ guiding me, I wouldn't be where I am today. Not in my career, nor in my life. No way. I foolishly tried it the other way relying on my own talent and foresight, and failed miserably. Whether it's writing a feature story, a gut wrenching crime report, or anchoring, relying on God, allows me to do it in a way that I never could on my own. Don't know how He does it, but thank goodness He does. "But for the grace of God go I"...a mystery, a blessing of faith.

KEVIN OGLE

KFOR Channel 4 News Anchor
Oklahoma City, OK

WE LIVE BY FAITH, NOT BY SIGHT.

2 CORINTHIANS 5:7

I *felt* the blast when a bomb tore the face off the Alfred P. Murrah Federal Building in Oklahoma City, killing 168 people and injuring hundreds more. I was too close to hear it. I walked away with no injuries but thought I was going to die from the pain.

On April 19, 1995, I was a young lawyer enjoying my first job as a Staff Attorney for a sentencing commission. I was seated at my desk, reviewing criminal statutes, which is very boring work. I had planned to take a break at 9:00 a.m. As I got up from my desk, the guy in the office behind me started chatting. That annoying encounter probably saved my life.

The blast of the bomb at 9:02 made my hair stand straight on end and threw me to the floor. *Something evil had happened.*

It was difficult getting out of the building. Everyone in my office went to the hospital, but I was not injured physically. Mentally, that is a different story.

After two days of being in shock, it hit me—the *horror*, the *despair*, the *hopelessness*, the *darkness*. It was as if the final shock wave from the bomb had come through and knocked me down again. And so began the darkest period of my life.

I am a strong person, and have overcome much in my life, but this was unbearable. I couldn't sleep. I couldn't think straight. I couldn't function. People told me I had been spared for a reason and I needed to move on. But I wasn't worthy.

I became bulimic. I didn't deserve to eat.

I went to church and cried through the service. I wasn't worthy of being there.

I realize now that I suffered from Post-Traumatic Stress Disorder, bulimia, and survivor guilt. But at the time it was just…darkness.

My mom, ever my caregiver and champion, would not give up. She took me to grief groups, counselors, doctors, church—but nothing worked.

Then we visited my grandmother's priest, Father Jack Feehily. I wasn't Catholic at the time, but my mother was desperate.

There was something about this man that I opened up to. I confided in him. I told him about the darkness I felt. Going to church made it worse. I told him I had been tested and had failed. *I had no faith.*

He looked at me with such compassion, told me that I needed to keep going to church. He didn't know if it would be weeks, or months, or even years, but that I would once again have faith and I would once again feel God's loving presence.

He took my hand, looked me in the eye, and said, "I have faith enough for both of us."

It was a turning point in my life. It was okay that I didn't have any faith, because his faith was strong enough to carry us both. He knew God hadn't abandoned me and that God would find His way back into my heart. He knew I would come out of the darkness because he had that much faith…in Him.

Father Feehily was right. His faith *was* strong enough for both of us. It began my journey out of darkness and back into light. And back to my faith.

MELISSA McLAWHORN HOUSTON

Former Attorney General's Office and Oklahoma Labor Commissioner
Norman, OK

I HAVE COME TO SEE
PRAYER
AS A PRIVILEGE,
NOT A DUTY.
LIKE ALL GOOD THINGS,
PRAYER REQUIRES
SOME DISCIPLINE. YET
I BELIEVE THAT
LIFE WITH GOD
SHOULD SEEM MORE LIKE
FRIENDSHIP
THAN DUTY.

PHILIP YANCEY
Prayer

BE STRONG AND COURAGEOUS.
DO NOT BE AFRAID OR TERRIFIED BECAUSE OF THEM,
FOR THE LORD YOUR GOD GOES WITH YOU;
HE WILL NEVER LEAVE YOU NOR FORSAKE YOU.

DEUTERONOMY 31:8

I grew up in the church, was baptized at Falls Creek Church Camp when I was 14, and married my sweetheart, Brad Henry, when I was 21. God was good. I was good. While I practiced the Christian faith with great discipline, I wouldn't say my faith was deep. My life had been relatively easy with lots of support from family and friends in Shawnee. Never could I have imagined the avalanche of sorrow and pain that awaited Brad and me in the coming days of our marriage.

I was so excited when we first became pregnant. I told everyone. Life was going just as we had planned. Soon, though, there was a miscarriage and I was devastated. Little did I know.

In time, I got pregnant again. This time the pregnancy continued and, to our amazement, we learned that there were two babies. Eight months after conception, we had two infant girls: Lindsey and Leah. They were perfect.

Eight weeks later, we noticed that Lindsey was not moving around in her crib like her sister. The doctor started tests. Two weeks later, we were called into his office to hear these words: "Your baby will not live to see her first birthday and we don't know about the other baby, you'll have to wait and see if she develops any symptoms."

We walked out of that office, numb with grief. There are no words to describe that time. Crying, on our knees, exhausted, caring for a sick baby and a healthy one. Begging God for a miracle.

Four months later Lindsey died in my arms. Why? Maybe God wasn't present or maybe it was my fault. What about the miracles of the Bible? Why hadn't there been a miracle for Lindsey?

For a time, there was just darkness and grief. Finally, some words from Father Mike, the president of St. Gregory's, brought me a little peace. He said maybe it wasn't Lindsey's life on earth that was meant to be, but her soul in heaven. That just gave me something to hold on to, as God held on to me. Even when I couldn't sense God's presence, He was there …giving me courage, helping me cope. Sometimes, simply living is brave determination.

Meanwhile, Leah continued to be in good health. Taking care of her was life saving for me. *Then*, the unheard of happened. Six months after Lindsey's death, I became pregnant again. There was a prenatal test for spinal muscular atrophy, which had been Lindsey's issue, but we chose not to have it. I was so scared. I remember crying out to God, saying, "I can't do this." We knew that Leah was okay, but would we watch every little movement of this new baby for a year to see if she was going to live? God help me. The anxiety was debilitating.

Laynie was born and, as I lay there after her birth, great peace and calm came over me. I actually felt a physical hug, yet nobody was there. I knew God was telling me that this daughter was okay. And she was. Today she is a missionary.

Losing a child isn't something you get over, but you can go on with life by the grace of God. During those early days, growing up in Shawnee, I certainly never expected to undergo such tragedy, but then I never expected to grow such deep faith either, or have the opportunity to become the First Lady of Oklahoma. God *is* good and faithful and will sustain us in the worst and best of times.

KIM HENRY

Executive Director, Sarkey's Foundation and Former First Lady of Oklahoma
Shawnee, OK

SEEK YE FIRST THE KINGDOM OF GOD, AND HIS RIGHTEOUSNESS;
AND ALL THESE THINGS SHALL BE ADDED UNTO YOU.

MATTHEW 6:33

I knew this was going to be a special day, but I had no idea how it would turn out. It's 4:30 a.m. I'm in Dallas speaking with a great team of people for Bill Glass Prison Ministries. My first opportunity to share that day was at a juvenile unit of young men. I watched the group of skinny boys shuffle into the room responding begrudgingly to the sharp barks of the guards. The air was chilled by the cold stares of boys whose innocence was long lost to fatherlessness, dysfunctional family life, abuse, violence, and more. So I threw myself in with all the energy I could muster… and nothing happened. Then I started sharing my story of growing up in a single parent household, and being fatherless and reaching out to my dad to connect with him at the encouragement of my wife. The air warmed and countenances softened and the young men leaned forward. I could see the spirit of God moving way beyond my ability to connect to these young men. All too soon it was over, the follow up team moved in and after a few handshakes and brief hugs I was rushed out to head to my next assignment. I heard the door of the jail open behind me and I turned to see the warden. She thanked me profusely for speaking to the boys and invited me to come back any time and told me that one young man that had been particularly difficult for them to reach had been deeply impacted by the message shared that morning. I thanked her for letting me know. I knew that it was only a few loving relationships in my life and God's grace that kept me from the same fate as those boys. In spite of some hard times, I was able to graduate from Cushing High School and play basketball for the University of Arkansas.

As I was leaving Dallas, a quick look at my cell phone revealed a call from my family. I knew something must be wrong. A series of calls revealed that my mom had just suffered an aneurysm; this was especially alarming to me because to my knowledge my Mom had never professed a relationship with Christ.

Mom was larger than life. Complicated but not sophisticated, humorous but serious, fun but intense at times, smart but not much education, she had presence and was liked and loved by many. She raised the five of us through sheer will power and hard work. I had been praying for her salvation since I was a boy, often fasting for her to know Jesus. And now I was a plane flight away, sharing the Gospel with others and she was on her deathbed.

As soon as I arrived in Oklahoma City, I called my sister. "Stephan, Mama didn't make it," she said.

I walked into the emergency room where my mom was still lying. A conversation with the neurosurgeon explained that there was no brain activity and she was gone. There were a lot of tears in that moment with my siblings and extended family and then my sister said, "Stephan, Mama accepted Christ shortly before she was brought to Oklahoma City." What? I almost jumped through the ceiling! My sister continued, "After the CAT Scan I said, 'Mama, Stephan said there is power in the name of Jesus. Let's just say Jesus and we did over and over again'. When we stopped, I ask her if she wanted to accept Him and she said 'yes!'" Some of the last words I know that my mom said was, "from this day forward I want to live my life for Christ," shortly after that the aneurysm took over and she lost consciousness.

Following a wonderful memorial, we made our way home. I was going through a mountain of mail and as I was reading the newsletter from Bill Glass Prison Ministries my eye caught my name in the letter. Bill recounted the story of the young man being touched by the message that I shared at the exact same time that God was using a traumatic health crisis to bring my mom to Himself. Bill Glass' letter closed with these words. "Isn't it true that when we take care of the things that concern God that He takes care of those things that concern us?"

STEPHAN MOORE

Leadership Staff, Kanakuk Kamps and Director, Shiloh Camp
Cushing/Oklahoma City, OK

I HAVE TOLD YOU THESE THINGS, SO THAT IN ME YOU MAY HAVE PEACE.
IN THIS WORLD YOU WILL HAVE TROUBLE.
BUT TAKE HEART! I HAVE OVERCOME THE WORLD.

JOHN 16:33

I felt like I had been punched in the stomach. All the air had been knocked out of my being. Those three little words turned my world upside down. YOU HAVE CANCER! That's something that happens to other people; older people, not me! I was 41 years old with two children, a loving husband, and an amazing career as a television news anchor. I didn't have time to have cancer. I remember thinking there must be some mistake. I had no history of breast cancer in my family. Then the reality hit me. You could die. YOU COULD DIE!

I immediately talked with my family and realized I had to develop a plan of attack. So I dried my tears and got to work. I called all the prayer warriors that I knew and told them to begin praying. I went to the elders of my church and asked them to anoint me with oil as described in the Bible. I began listening to scriptures about healing. I began to saturate my spirit with God's word. I had been raised in church and attended Oral Roberts University so I had been taught about putting on the whole armor of God. But never was I more aware of having the Sword of the Spirit, the word of God to help in this battle. At every turn, I called upon the Lord's word to fight the enemy.

God brought so many wonderful people into my life during this journey. One in particular reminded me that what the devil meant for evil, God would turn for good. It was at that moment I had a peace, that passed all earthly understanding. I knew God was going to be with me during this battle.

After surgery, chemotherapy, and radiation, my healing was complete.

111

That diagnosis was back in 2003. I'm reminded daily that God has given me a purpose and a platform to share my story. I talk with women weekly about their health. I encourage them to get their mammograms and see their doctor on a regular basis. I help them find services that will get them the answers they need.

I feel God has blessed me with this opportunity to help others. I would never have wished to have breast cancer, but I see now that it's one of the best things that's ever happened to me. I never take anyone or anything for granted. I live in the moment. I love deeply. I laugh and smile and know that God is bigger than anything this world can throw my way. Maybe you are in the midst of your own challenge and it seems dark and hopeless. I know otherwise. Whatever you're going through, God is there too!

LeAnne Taylor

KOTV Channel 6 News Anchor
Tulsa, OK

"FOR MY THOUGHTS ARE NOT YOUR THOUGHTS,
NEITHER ARE YOUR WAYS MY WAYS," DECLARES THE LORD.
"AS THE HEAVENS ARE HIGHER THAN THE EARTH,
SO ARE MY WAYS HIGHER THAN YOUR WAY
AND MY THOUGHTS THAN YOUR THOUGHTS."

ISAIAH 55: 8-9

I am an experimental particle physicist doing research with some of the most sophisticated and complex equipment ever built by humans, studying the most fundamental particles and forces that make up the universe. It's an awesome, exciting, and fun career. But I might have been a theologian.

When I was born, my dad was working on a Doctor of Theology degree at Dallas Theological Seminary (DTS). Upon hearing the news of my birth, John Walvoord, the president of DTS, sent a letter to my parents guaranteeing me admission into seminary when I was old enough to attend. During my senior year of college I still did not know what I wanted to do in life, or where God might be calling me, but with that letter in hand, and excellent grades, I applied to DTS. Because I liked physics I also applied to five graduate schools in physics. I didn't know if I would be accepted into graduate school in physics, but I did know that I would be accepted into DTS. Except, I wasn't.

In my application letter to DTS I stated honestly that I did not know whether or not God was calling me into professional Christian ministry, but I was considering that option. Unbeknownst to me, the previous year the seminary had set up a policy that only applicants who *knew* God was calling them into professional Christian ministry would be accepted, and because I was not sure, I was rejected, despite my letter from Dr. Walvoord. Dallas Seminary only retained that policy for two years, so clearly God didn't want me to attend there the year I applied. I have often wondered who God didn't want attending the other year DTS had that policy.

But God's direction didn't end with closing the door to seminary. As the famous radio personality Paul Harvey used to say, you have to hear "the rest of the story."

Of the five schools I applied to for graduate work in physics I got accepted to two of them and decided to attend UCLA. The very first day of my first class at UCLA the professor began by reviewing a topic that every first year graduate student in physics should know, but I had never seen before. That seemed strange to me because I had taken classes covering the four basic subjects in physics that are needed to get into graduate school. However, I began to ask some fellow students about their preparation for physics graduate school. What I learned was shocking! Every other student had taken each of the four basic physics subjects twice, once in lower division classes and once in upper division classes. However, because my major was not a Physics major, but a Physical Science major, I had only taken each of the basic subjects once at the lower division level. I was about one year of classes deficient in my preparation for physics graduate school!

I quickly realized that I could not succeed as a graduate student in physics without the proper prerequisites so I decided to talk with the graduate advisor about my situation. I went into his office and told him that I had only taken lower division physics classes as an undergraduate student. He was astonished and bluntly asked, "How did you get in here?" Those words still ring in my ears today. I sheepishly said something like, "I must have had good grades" but I was actually thinking, "Wow, God must have really wanted me to be here!"

You see, by any human criteria, I should have easily been accepted to DTS and quickly been rejected from UCLA. But God is not limited by human criteria. It is trivial for him to close doors that should be open and open doors that should be closed. He moves kings' hearts, and graduate application committees' as well. Are you doubting that God can open and close doors for you? Are you doubting that God can do something in your life today that might seem impossible? I encourage you to change that doubt to trust. God is true to his word when he says, "all things are possible" (Matthew 19:26). My career as a particle physicist is testimony to that very fact!

DR. MICHAEL G. STRAUSS, PH.D.

Author and David Ross Boyd Professor of Physics, University of Oklahoma
Norman, OK

FOR I KNOW THE PLANS I HAVE FOR YOU, SAYS THE LORD.
THEY ARE PLANS FOR GOOD AND NOT FOR DISASTER,
TO GIVE YOU A FUTURE AND A HOPE.

JEREMIAH 29:11

We are told that fire *drills* should be planned—not a surprise. Then, in the case of a real fire, we instinctively, without thought, do what we have practiced. Faith, I believe, is very similar. Life had been good to us, our four children, their spouses, and grandchildren. Yet, in the blink of an eye, our world was shattered. *Instinctively*, and *without thought*, my faith guided my response.

It began February 15, 2011, when our son, Oklahoma City Police Officer Chad Peery, was assaulted while trying to protect others. The assault left him a quadriplegic, paralyzed from the collarbone down. Without feeling or ability to move, Chad now faced a life dependent on others for every movement and bodily function—except thought and speech. Like others might feel faced with that reality, Chad wished that he had not survived. Those were the most devastating moments, then days, weeks, months of my life, as a mother. How do you help your child face the total loss of life, as he knew it, and a future incomprehensible?

Chad was not expected to live through that first night. However, after two weeks, two surgeries, and much prayer, he was stable enough to move to rehab. Late one night, Chad lay there, unable to move. He began to cry, "Mama, I didn't deserve this … and I am trying hard not to be bitter." Through my own tears and heartbreak, I assured him that he didn't deserve it and that he had every right to be bitter. "However", I said, "if you accept that bitterness….if you focus on what you have lost, and what evil took from you it will eat you up. And evil will take that much more from you." Little did I realize that those words would push him—all of us—during his difficult journey over the next two years.

There is a quote that says, "If what's ahead scares you and what's behind hurts you, just look above, He never fails to help you." Another that says, "When you have come to the edge of all light that you know, and are about to drop off into the darkness of the unknown, Faith is knowing one of two things will happen: There will be something solid to stand on, or you will be taught to fly."

Well, Chad was killed in a tragic car accident two years after his assault. So, what's behind, and now ahead without our son, hurts more than can be put into words. And, it has definitely felt at times that I am about to drop off into darkness. I know prayers from so many people have held us up. And I know without a doubt the prayers help me put one foot in front of the other and face life one step at a time.

Repeatedly from the first fateful night, people said, "don't ask why." For me, the "why" was never in question. It was evil that made our son a quadriplegic and began that journey that ultimately took his life, not God. But, I believe it was God that gave Chad the spirit and will to fight for survival. God brought so very many people into Chad's life to help him, and our family, survive. God used Chad, as he displayed unimaginable courage and determination in the face of his devastation, to inspire others—many we will never know. In countless ways, *God brought good* from what evil began.

I believe that my God gives only good to His children. I claim that scripture from Jeremiah 29, God gives me hope—hope that eventually the pain will subside and the confidence that He will sustain me *through* the pain.

This journey has reinforced to me that we must learn to live life's journey with courage, integrity, purpose, and faith. We must be willing to let go of the life we have planned so as to have the life that God has waiting for us. We must live and practice our faith in the good times, so that in those moments when we need it, our faith instinctively, without thought, leads us through the fire.

JAN PEERY

President, YWCA
Oklahoma City, OK

116

CAST ALL YOUR ANXIETIES ON HIM BECAUSE HE CARES FOR YOU.

1 PETER 5:7

On the wall of my office is a black-and-white photograph of a tall, rough-hewn army officer and a stocky man in a business suit. The notation on the back reads "Bellingham, Washington, 1946".

Like most who have spent years in elective office, I have a multitude of photos on my wall of presidents, governors, and sports heroes. But this lone photograph of two seemingly unimportant men is the one I treasure most. It is my spiritual heritage.

After World War II, the founder of The Navigators, Dawson Trotman, sent his right-hand man to Seattle, Washington, to start a military ministry. Several weeks later, when Trotman checked to see how things were going, Lorne Sanny reported that he had started a Bible study. When asked how many men were coming to the study, Sanny admitted that only one man was attending—a young lieutenant named Charlie Riggs. Trotman paused, and then said, "Major on Riggs!"

Ten years later, in 1956, when Billy Graham came to Oklahoma City for a month-long crusade, Sanny and Riggs came as a part of Graham's team. My father, Jack Humphreys, went to the crusade the first evening. Dad had signed up to be an usher and intended to get the lay of the land the first evening, and then delegate the responsibility to other men from his church so he would not have to attend every night. Dad had no idea that God would use that first evening to change his life.

My father met Charlie Riggs that evening. Charlie was a former oil field roustabout and was anything but smooth, but the way he served people with a smile on his face and a spring in his step caught Dad's attention.

Dad decided to come back the next night to find out what made Charlie Riggs tick. As they worked together setting up chairs, Charlie began asking Dad questions about his relationship with Jesus Christ—When did he read the Bible? How often did he pray? Did he ever have a "quiet time?" Dad admitted that he read the Bible when he prepared a Sunday School lesson, prayed when he was in trouble, and had no idea what a quiet time was.

Dad had been a Christian for many years, but he had never matured in his walk with Christ. He attended church regularly, tithed, and taught a Sunday School class, but his purpose in life was to become wealthy. It was as if he had made a deal to give Sundays to God, but kept the other six days to pursue his dream of becoming a millionaire by age 40. Dad's plan wasn't working out very well. He owned a small chain of five-and-dime stores, was losing money, and was deep in debt.

Dad went back every night of the month-long crusade. He was searching for real answers to life's problems, and Charlie Riggs seemed to have the answers. After Billy Graham left town, Charlie continued to keep in touch with Dad, encouraging him and helping him learn how to grow in his faith day by day.

Several months later, Charlie called one day to ask if Dad could meet with him the following week. Dad cleared his schedule and Charlie spent an afternoon with him. Later Dad learned that Charlie had driven hundreds of miles to spend the day with him and another man in Oklahoma City, Gene Warr. Dad asked Charlie why he was willing to do that in order to help him. Charlie responded, "Jack, my work with Mr. Graham requires me to be away from my family most of the time. I've told God that I'm willing to pay that price if He will give me one man in each city into whom I can pour my life. In Oklahoma City He gave me two—you and Gene."

The Bible says "any man who is in Christ is a new creation." That was certainly true with my father. Though I was only 6 years old at the time, I noticed the change. One day I asked my mother, "Mom, how come Dad doesn't yell at me anymore?" My Dad's new relationship with Jesus Christ changed his temperament, his habits, and even his goals in life.

Dad's business, however, continued to struggle. He had trouble trusting God to meet his financial needs, believing that his own greed had led to his problems and he would need to work his way out of them. One day a friend challenged him to consider the promise of God in I Peter 5:7, "Cast all your anxieties on him, because he cares for you." Dad began to see that God was able to meet all of his needs—even his seemingly insurmountable financial problems.

Over the next few years, Dad sold all of his retail stores and began a new wholesale distribution company. One day he got a call asking him to sell sewing notions to the base exchange at Tinker Air Force Base. Apparently he met a need for the exchange service; within a few months he was supplying Army and Air Force exchanges from border to border. It took Dad five years to pay off all of his debts. After eight more years he retired as a millionaire at age 49!

After retirement, Dad spent 26 years as a part-time volunteer helping Charlie Riggs train counselors for Billy Graham Crusade across the United States, Canada, and Australia. Mom traveled with him, and it was the richest experience of their lives.

What difference can one life make?

Dawson Trotman helped Lorne Sanny grow in his relationship with Jesus Christ. Lorne Sanny had only one serviceman in his Bible study—Charlie Riggs. Charlie Riggs asked God to give him one man in each city where Billy Graham held a crusade. Fifty-nine years ago in Oklahoma City, Charlie helped Gene Warr and Jack Humphreys. Gene and Dad touched untold thousands of lives in Oklahoma City and around the world.

I am one whose life has been profoundly changed. And that's why I have that picture on my wall of Lorne Sanny and his one-man Bible study, Charlie Riggs.

KIRK HUMPHREYS

Chairman, The Humphreys Company and Former Mayor of Oklahoma City
Oklahoma City, OK

I AM DEFINITELY GOING **TO GIVE SOME** TO MY CHURCH. BECAUSE THEY ARE ALWAYS RAISING MONEY FOR DIFFERENT **MISSIONS** AND MISSION PROGRAMS. AND SECOND, I HAVE TO GIVE **MY MOM** A DISHWASHER BECAUSE WE DEFINITELY NEED MORE HOUSEHOLD APPLIANCES.

DARCI LYNNE FARMER, AGE 12
Winner of *America's Got Talent*
Responding to the question: "What will you do
with the million-dollar prize?"

BUT THE HELPER, THE HOLY SPIRIT, WHOM THE FATHER WILL SEND
IN MY NAME, HE WILL TEACH YOU ALL THINGS AND BRING TO YOUR
REMEMBRANCE ALL THAT I HAVE SAID TO YOU.

JOHN 14:26

Even before I was 10 years of age, I told my mother and father that I wanted to be a medical doctor. My father, a practicing dentist in Oklahoma City for some 50 years, was disappointed because he wanted me to follow in his footsteps. I continued to keep that goal in mind and at 18 years of age, at Falls Creek Baptist Assembly near Davis, Oklahoma, I dedicated my life to become a medical missionary to China.

For some reason, China always attracted me. However, it was not until 1988 that I went for the first time and was shocked to see the living conditions and third world experience of the China country. In Beijing, they had very few paved roads and the only use of those roads was for the military and literally millions of people were riding bicycles. They had no modern highways, there were rundown office buildings, and yes, the air pollution was already there.

But over the next 30 years, I have had the privilege of returning to China for both professional business and nationwide tours. On a business trip to Beijing in 2012, I had the privilege of speaking at a large university and sharing the platform with the previously retired Vice Minister of Health. I shared my experience that I had in 1988 with the condition of Beijing in 2012. There were modern 100-story buildings, superhighways with express lanes, and thousands of Audis (their national car), Mercedes Benz, and General Motors vehicles (more sold in China than the United States). No longer did they ride bicycles, but motorcycles and motorbikes, nearly 50% of the people were smokers, and there was a fast food American restaurant on nearly every corner.

I shared with the former Vice Minister of Health the comparison of the U.S.

and Chinese. Due to a forthcoming presentation in China, my study revealed that approximately 13% of their children and 33% of their adults were overweight or obese, about the same statistics of obesity that we had in the United States in 1990. But since 1990, we had grown to 33% of our children being overweight or obese and 67% of our adults. I pointed out that our health care in 1990 was $700-billion and in 2012, almost $3-trillion. Also, I told him that even though the U.S. spends twice as much money on health care as any country in the world (an average of $8,000 per person) our longevity ranked 42nd worldwide. I told him that I was convinced that we spend way too much of our health service dollars on desperate measures which often prolongs death, not life, only for a few days.

In comparing what had happened in the United States since 1990 and the change in lifestyle in China during that periodic of time, I thought they were seeing a "perfect storm," to have the same problem that we have in 22 years. The Vice Minister of Health agreed with my prediction and he asked, "Can you help?"

Following that experience in Beijing in 2012, I was asked to return to Hainan, China in 2013 and participate in an "economic forum" concentrating on Asia. While there, I spoke to a large group of dignitaries from several Southeast Asia countries and also was privileged to be in a group who met with President Xi Jinping who had recently been selected to become the new president. I was told that he had a personal interest in trying to improve the health and fitness of all Chinese people, but particularly the youth, as I have been trying to do in this country over the past 45 years.

We have looked at several possibilities of signing contracts with the Chinese for both the improvement of health and fitness among Chinese people and to avoid the health crisis that has overwhelmed the United States over the past 2½ decades—and things are happening!

In April 2017, I was invited to speak in Beijing to a large group of businessman and members of the Communist Party. The topic was "Cooper Aerobics for a Healthy China by 2030." (They selected the date, I would be 99 years of age but my son Tyler, age 47, is following in my footsteps.) Upon completion of the presentation, I signed a contract to help them achieve that goal.

In October 2018, I was asked to return to China (my 12th visit) and give a series of presentations at Vitalake 45 minutes from downtown Beijing. It is more of a resort community on a 1,000-acre lake. Their emphasis is on preventive medicine and wellness, concentrating on children. There are plans for a Cooper Aerobics Park where people will use exercise as a means not only of preventing disease, but even treating it. Already they have medically supervised programs to manage high blood pressure, diabetes and obesity. And, we are discussing the possibility of having a Cooper Preventive Medical Clinic on that campus!

I have had the opportunity to attend lunches and dinners with some of the very successful and wealthy businessmen in China. On one of these occasions, I asked Mr. David Dai, with whom I had been working in China, if I could pray and bless that food which is my custom. He responded favorably and from then on, I had multiple meetings with these very successful Chinese businessmen and not only did I pray to bless the food, but also prayed to improve the relationships between the United States and China. My host said later that, "Your interest in the health of the Chinese people, and particularly the children, did more to improve the relationships between the two countries than did 30 years of political activity."

In considering the experiences I have had in my twelve trips to China, it finally dawned upon me that I am a medical missionary to China; but contrary to working in a small rural hospital which I thought was my calling, I have been asked to work with 1.3-billion Chinese people.

In conclusion, God had a plan for me from these early years, but it was far more than I expected to be doing. My only question is…at 87 years of age, why did the Lord wait so long?

KENNETH H. COOPER, MD, MPH

Founder, The Cooper Institute and Cooper Clinic, Author,
and Oklahoma Hall of Fame Inductee
Oklahoma City, OK/Dallas, TX

YOU WILL KEEP IN PERFECT PEACE THOSE WHOSE MINDS
ARE STEADFAST, BECAUSE THEY TRUST IN YOU.

ISAIAH 26:3

Moments race by and are never thought of again. In fact, that is the cadence for most moments during any given day. And then there are others, which are seared into your soul never to be forgotten. When they later come to mind it is as if the experience had just happened—you remember the particulars with a knowing intensity. The environment, the smells, your clothing, and more, rise up in full detail. When those moments occur, I believe God is directing us to stop and recognize the sacredness of that moment. Maybe it is the chance to know Him a little deeper.

One of those sacred moments found its way to me, when all distractions were whisked away and my focus was solely, fervently, and genuinely tuned into the present moment. My father passed away. It was a call I expected to receive for years, and yet when it came I was taken aback. Ours was an extraordinarily complex relationship, one that often left me confused, sad, and feeling lonely. And yet, I always yearned for a nearness that was simply not to be during our lifetimes.

After a tumultuous relationship, my parents divorced when I was only three years old. My father led a rollercoaster life, which included nine marriages. He only popped into my life every three to five years, often unannounced. Birthdays were neglected, his only grandchild's birth overlooked, and on and on. As we both aged, I heard through the "grapevine" he was in an assisted living center. I visited, and while he seemed happy to see me I couldn't find the storybook father I longed for. And if I'm vulnerable and honest, I didn't visit often.

When I heard the words "he is gone," time stood still. Apologies, notions of "I'll get to it tomorrow," or seeing him the following weekend were no longer an option. When I was young, *he* decided the sporadic nature of our relationship, but as his body and mind faded, that choice had become mine. Now, I was forced to face all the ways I could have done things differently. My soul felt the deeply painful nudge of sorrow and deep regret.

The day of his funeral my brother and I drove to a rural cemetery in western Oklahoma. During the graveside service, I cried rivers of tears amongst people I barely knew. When I regained my composure, I stood beside his casket and gently held his cold hand as time once again stood still. The weight of recognizing our time had passed was heavy. Regrets were to be forever unresolved and words never again spoken. Then a deep knowing rose up in my heart…*we both had done our best.* A peace that truly passed all understanding engulfed me in an instant.

Saying so long in a tiny, country cemetery offered me an unexpected space to unequivocally know while ours was an unconventional father-daughter relationship, it was just that: ours. And no matter what transgressions had transpired while he was alive, we were family. Forgiveness flooded my heart and I knew he forgave me, as I forgave him. I'll never know exactly what occurred in that moment, but I can say for certain God was centermost of the enduring peace I feel today.

TISHA TATE

Vice President of Commercial Development, Delaware Resource Group (DRG)
and Yoga Instructor
Elk City/Oklahoma City, OK

NO TEMPTATION HAS OVERTAKEN YOU EXCEPT WHAT IS COMMON TO
MANKIND. AND GOD IS FAITHFUL;
HE WILL NOT LET YOU BE TEMPTED BEYOND WHAT YOU CAN BEAR.
BUT WHEN YOU ARE TEMPTED, HE WILL ALSO PROVIDE A WAY OUT
SO THAT YOU CAN ENDURE IT.
THEREFORE, MY DEAR FRIENDS, FLEE FROM IDOLATRY.

1 CORINTHIANS 10:13-14

I am a believer delivered from Drug Addiction, my name is Glen.
I am 57, married 27 years. I have a 30-year-old son and a 15-year-old daughter.

Now I will start my story by telling you that for years and years as a child and adult I had a large hole in my heart. This hole caused me lots of pain, bitterness, sadness, and unhappiness. My answer was to always try and fill this hole with the ways of the world not the ways of the Lord.

Now, don't get me wrong, I knew who the Lord was and as an eighth-grader accepted Jesus Christ as my Lord and Savior. That didn't last long for me. I did the same thing again at the age of 18. I went back into the ways of the world after about three months. Lucky for me the Holy Spirit would stay with me and attempt to help me, only I thought I knew better.

The Lord protected me countless times from death and self-destruction and I do mean that literally. I was dealing and using drugs all day every day. At the peak of my addiction I used insane amounts of drugs.

I am proud to say that I have not used hard drugs for over 33 years. What I am not proud to tell you is that although I was able, with the help of Jesus Christ, to quit using hard drugs, I was a "pot head" until the summer of 2002 when by the grace and mercy of God; he delivered me from this desire.

Since 1987, I have pretty much lived a life of good works and have been a productive, not destructive, citizen. My good works did not include attending church, praying, or reading the Bible. I rarely attended church, almost never read my Bible, and would only pray in times of NEED!!! After all, why should I do these things; I am a good person, I have a great wife, good job, nice home, nice cars, and good kids. Why do I need God? You know I did have some happiness, some good times. What I did *not* have was peace or joy in my life, nor was my life to be considered abundant; it took things and events to make that happiness. It would not last very long. I still had this large hole in my heart…

In 2002 I finally decided to fill that large hole in my heart with the one and only thing capable of filling it. I chose to give my Heart, Soul, Mind, and Strength to my Lord Jesus Christ.

During the last 16 years, my life has changed so drastically and wonderfully I really don't know where to begin. The Lord has turned an ugly sickness into a wonderful gift—a completely transformed life. I now enjoy reading and studying my Bible, prayer time, and telling others of the wonders of Jesus Christ. God has showed me that to have a life of abundance it will have to include Him. With God in my life I now realize all things are truly possible and it does not take things, events, or other people to bring me joy and peace in my life. My happiness comes through living one day at a time with my Lord and Savior.

Over ten years ago, I shared with God the plan I had to start my own ministry, a 12-step program that acknowledged Jesus Christ as the one and only healing power in our lives.

This prayer led my wife and me to California to visit a Ministry called Celebrate Recovery. We went to Saddleback Church in March of 2003 where the presence of the Holy Spirit and God's healing powers were everywhere. It was obvious the Lord was showing me something very special.

What I learned from this Ministry was that anybody could be helped who was humble enough to admit they were not perfect and needed help understanding God's grace and his healing powers in their lives. This ministry also helps you understand what God's will is for you; and gives you the strength to live in His will instead of your own.

It's easy to look back now and see God positioning me for his plan. Recently, I celebrated 11½ years of ministry and 10 years of employment with my church, leading this incredible ministry in Oklahoma. God has not wasted any of the pain in my life; instead He has used it to bring about healing for others.

GLEN GRUSENDORF, JR.

Director of Recovery Ministries, Asbury United Methodist Church
Tulsa, OK

AND WHAT DOES THE LORD REQUIRE OF YOU?
TO ACT JUSTLY AND TO LOVE MERCY AND
TO WALK HUMBLY WITH YOUR GOD.

MICAH 6:8

My first memories of my home in Viet Nam were of a straw hut with no inside toilet or kitchen, a dirt floor, and no one had separate bedrooms. My mother worked very long days in the rice fields and would often go without food so she could bring her lunch home for us kids to eat. The village we lived in was incredibly poor, and my family was constantly afraid of the communist Vietnamese who were now in power.

Our father fought against the communists alongside the United States Military and was forced to leave for America after the fall of Saigon in 1975. Life was hard for everyone in our village, but especially for those of us who had ties to the United States. If you were suspected of any allegiance to America, the soldiers would either burn your home down or arrest you and make you attend a reform school.

When my dad left, my mother was supporting two young children and was five months pregnant with me. Our lives were extremely tough, but coming to America when I was eleven years old was even tougher. Little did I know it would become the biggest blessing of my life—the gateway to an amazing future that would have been impossible in my native country of Viet Nam.

When my family and I arrived in America, we joined our father in Yukon, Oklahoma. We didn't speak a word of English and this lack of speaking the English language made people think we were not very smart. When it came to mathematics, however, I discovered I could communicate with numbers and was quick to learn. I learned English quickly and never was required to attend any special classes. My teachers recognized the skills I had and it began to bolster my confidence and open my eyes to the future I could achieve.

I loved school, it provided many encouraging people and safety. Education was everything to me and I was given the opportunity to attend Oklahoma State University and, later, Oklahoma City University Law School.

These hard times built a certain toughness in me, and I am resilient because I know what I have overcome. God uses my prior experiences to give me a great deal of compassion toward others. As a District Judge, I have been able to work in the Criminal Justice system and the Oklahoma County Jail to bring families back together. I know what it is like to live in extreme poverty. I personally know how it feels and what it means to have families torn apart.

Today, there are thousands of people in Oklahoma who are in jail because they have no money. Many may be there for months and months. Consider what this means for their families: They lose their job, their car, perhaps their home, and many times the families are torn apart. This may be true even though they have not committed a bad crime or were violent. These individuals are in jail without being formally charged with or convicted of any crime. They are detained in jail solely because they cannot afford the bond set by our court system. I go almost every weekend to the county jail to sign "own recognizance" bonds to allow people that can't afford a bond the opportunity to get into treatment and be successful. Additionally, this allows them to be with their families and to return to some semblance of a normal life while they submit to the criminal justice system.

I know that I am called to help others, and sometimes it is not easy. I am certainly not necessarily popular with some segments of the community, but by the grace of God I have survived a very difficult childhood and am blessed to live in this country, a land of opportunity. Believing in God has held me together through the rough times and has given me hope for my future and the future of others who need and deserve a second chance.

CINDY TRUONG

District 7 Judge, Oklahoma County
Viet Nam/Oklahoma City, OK

LORD, YOUR DISCIPLINE IS GOOD, FOR IT LEADS TO LIFE AND HEALTH.
YOU RESTORE MY HEALTH AND ALLOW ME TO LIVE!

ISAIAH 38:16

Growing up in western Oklahoma, I probably took lots of things for granted. My parents were honest, loving, and hard working people. I surely took that for granted as life introduces you to those with contrary values. Dinner at the same table, same time nearly every night. Conversations about your day and advice on how to handle challenges. We celebrated victories together and worked to solve life's problems together. The simplicity of rural Oklahoma also was not a topic that cried for attention. Life was simple. No traffic, ever. Very little crime, ever. Our focus seemed to be on a community of people. We, again, celebrated wins and struggled together with losses. Those most often came in the form of our high school sports teams or with a community member death.

As a youngster and later as a young man, I never really thought about not being healthy. I was, as were all of my three siblings, healthy. My parents were healthy. I was not even exposed to illness until my adulthood as I attended Oklahoma Baptist University. It was there that I began a job working for the local hospital pharmacy. I had many roles, but one was to deliver prescription medicine to local nursing homes. There were lots of older people, many suffering from disease and illness. I literally hated going to the nursing homes as seeing the suffering was so foreign. Fast forward 25 years and I too found myself suffering from an illness that was not escapable.

At the age of 46, I woke up with both hands frozen in claw shapes; my wrists were so swollen that I couldn't strap on my watch. I was diagnosed with a chronic disease that would most likely never go away. I went through all of the normal emotions. I was saddened. I was no longer able to be as physically active as I once was. I was angered. How could this happen? And, even more importantly, why did it happen? I struggled, in my own way, for months before realizing that my God is with me in all of my struggles and my victories. I began looking at things I could do to minimize the impact of the dreadful pain and discomfort of rheumatoid arthritis. Changing my diet radically was one change I believed would improve my condition. I forcused on eating healthy foods like fish and salads. I gave up bread, pasta, sweets, or anything with gluten. I even gave up sodas. For five years I was on a toxic nausea-and-fatigue-causing chemotherapy drug, but I was able to quit because of the changes I made in diet. I was even able to resume my love of mountain bike riding.

Along the way, I prayed to God for complete healing. I leaned on His word. One of my favorite verses became, "O Lord my God, I cried to you for help, and you restored my health." I had so few choices. My faith and my family were where I went for support. I now realize that what I took for granted in rural Oklahoma roots were so genuine and so real. But life changes and we are faced with the reality of making choices. Matthew 28:20 states, "Teach these new disciples to obey all the commands I have given you. And be sure of this: I am with you always, even to the end of the age." Wow. God's presence has made all the difference. But, I also know I am responsible for my body and how I take care of what God has given me. Those responsibilities include being in charge of my diet, my lifestyle, and my exercise.

Taking things for granted is natural, it seems. Even your health.

JIM GEBHART

President, Mercy Health System
Burns Flat/Oklahoma City, OK

PRAY AS THOUGH EVERYTHING DEPENDED ON GOD.
WORK AS THOUGH EVERYTHING DEPENDED ON YOU.

SAINT AUGUSTINE

I was blessed to grow up in a loving family in Stillwater, play professional golf, serve my country as a fighter pilot with three combat tours in Iraq, marry Jacqy, and be Dad to five incredible girls. In the midst of living a good life, everything changed one rainy night on a commercial flight through Chicago.

As I boarded the plane, I walked by a young soldier in dress greens sitting quietly in first class. *Probably home on leave*, I thought. I was glad someone had taken care of this young corporal.

After we landed, the captain announced to the passengers, "We are carrying the remains of Army Corporal Brock Bucklin …and his twin brother, Corporal Brad Bucklin, has brought him home from Iraq."

The captain went on to request that everyone remain seated as a sign of respect until Brock Bucklin's remains were removed from the aircraft. Tragically, not everyone honored that request.

For the next 30 minutes I watched out the window of the plane as this hero's ceremony unfolded. It was heartbreaking.

The Bucklin family stood on the tarmac, holding each other as a shield against the pain. And then it came, conveyed from the belly of our 737, wrapped in a finely pressed, carefully placed five-by-nine swath of red, white, and blue by way of Dover Air Force Base—the meaning of sacrifice.

As Brock Bucklin's flag-draped casket descended the cargo hold ramp, inch by final inch, his four-year-old son, Jacob, securely enveloped in the arms of his grandmother, could only watch. His young were eyes fixed on the casket of his father, who would never hold him again. Brock had given up that treasure, his very life, for the sake of every other father and son, in the name of the colors that now covered his body, his world all gone, so the rest of us can live free.

The dignified hands of the honor guard, sheathed in brilliant white gloves that shone in the darkness, were raised in honor over the brave warrior's remains. Brock had come home for the last time. His brother stood by his casket.

As I watched the Bucklin family facing such grief I couldn't help but wonder: *What if the tide of war turned on my family? What would their future be like without me?* I knew that Jacob and thousands like him would have to grow up without a parent to nurture and provide for them.

At that moment, I felt a powerful force calling me to action.

Walking off the plane and up the jet bridge, I knew God had given me a mission in life. I didn't know exactly what I was going to do or where I was going to start, but I knew I had to do something to help that family and others like them. Also, we all had to work to ensure that the sacrifices of America's heroes—our fallen military personnel—would never go unappreciated or unrewarded. God had been preparing me for this moment my whole life.

That was the beginning of a journey that today is Folds of Honor. It's an organization that has raised over $100 million and awarded over 13,000 educational scholarships to the family members of soldiers killed or disabled in combat. Patriot Golf Day is the primary way we raise funds. It has become the largest grass-roots golf fundraiser in America.

I've received lots of honor and attention for the work that's been done, but the true reward is the feeling of fulfillment from doing something for people like Jacob and his family. I thank God every morning for this opportunity to bless America and those who serve and sacrifice.

MAJOR DAN ROONEY, USAF

PGA Golf Professional, F-16 Fighter Pilot, and Founder & CEO, Folds of Honor
Owasso, OK

So, when the tumor returned for an encore in 2016, [Scott] Hamilton decided to react differently.

There was no 'Why me?'

anymore. 'I figured I needed to go through this with joy,' he said. 'It was just a muscle I needed to build, like the muscles I built skating.'

Juliet Macur

AND THE PEACE OF GOD, WHICH TRANSCENDS ALL UNDERSTANDING,
WILL GUARD YOUR HEARTS
AND YOUR MINDS IN CHRIST JESUS.

PHILIPPIANS 4:7

In the summer of 1992, my brother Jimmy passed away after a courageous battle with a rare childhood cancer. He was only 17 years old. Our family was plunged into a hole of grief.

People would approach me with tears streaming down their faces to offer comfort. I would hold them and say thank you, it was God's will for him. As I type this I still feel the peace and comfort in those words as I did then. The problem was, I did not consider that God had a will and plan for me.

Several years passed and I was no closer to feeling a personal connection with God in my life. A friend asked me if I would serve as her first child's Godmother. I agreed, all the while thinking I wasn't worthy of the title. The service was held in a small Episcopal church in Columbus, Ohio. I remember saying the responses, "I will with God's help" and how powerful that phrase sounded echoed in this small church.

That Sunday afternoon I boarded a plane to return back to Oklahoma City. Shortly after takeoff there was an explosion and the plane started to turn on its side. The screams of fear from my fellow passengers was deafening, I wouldn't want my worst enemies to have heard those noises.

Instead of panicking I grabbed a cross I wore around my neck. It was a gift from my dad after Jimmy had died. Immediately, I realized I wasn't in charge and couldn't go into the cockpit and save these people. I also remembered the mantra "I will with God's help" and suddenly I was calm.

While holding the cross, I had my first conversation with God. I told God that if I was supposed to go down in an airplane then I accepted my fate. Instantly, the sounds of the passengers muted and a glowing warmth enveloped me, I was in a peace which passeth understanding.

I added a request that God let my family know I loved them very much as I had not told them so in those darker years of grief and asked that He let them know that at this moment in time I was completely at peace. Something I had longed for from early years.

In the midst of this the pilots were able to gain control and we landed along a well-lit runway of emergency vehicles of all kind.

We had survived, but the experience for me was so much more.

At this time in my life, my friends were not very spiritual. I tried to explain the immense spiritual experience; all they heard was a hero story that I had survived a plane crash. It was easier to acquiesce and not talk about the God part.

By the grace of God a few years later I met new friends. These people heard the story and understood the meaning of the spiritual experience. Since then my conversations with God have only grown in importance and in practice. Should I spend each day trying to adhere to God's will for me, whatever it may be, I believe I will know Peace on Earth again, and in many ways I do.

TRICIA EVEREST

Attorney, Advisory Committee for Inasmuch Foundation, Philanthropist, and Community Volunteer
Oklahoma City, OK

DO NOT WORRY ABOUT YOUR LIFE,
WHAT YOU WILL EAT OR WHAT YOU WILL DRINK,
NOR ABOUT YOUR BODY, WHAT YOU WILL PUT ON.
WHICH OF YOU BY BEING ANXIOUS CAN ADD A SINGLE HOUR
TO HIS SPAN OF LIFE?
YOUR HEAVENLY FATHER KNOWS YOUR NEEDS;
SEEK FIRST THE KINGDOM OF GOD AND HIS RIGHTEOUSNESS,
AND ALL THESE THINGS WILL BE ADDED TO YOU.

FROM THE BOOK OF MATTHEW

I am an ophthalmologist, and have been in practice for more than 30 years. You can imagine over that period of time, I have had some memorable cases. You might enjoy reading further about one.

Many years ago, I was faced with an older diabetic requesting a surgical procedure for the cataract in her left eye; the vision in her right eye had been lost due to proliferative diabetic retinopathy. I felt obligated to be realistic with her. She already had one leg amputated below the knee, another sign of how devastating her diabetic disease was.

"I have to be honest with you, I believe the surgical procedure on the front part of your eye would be successful, but the probability is that the back of your eye is so affected by diabetic damage, that I cannot be certain that your vision will improve. I am reluctant to recommend surgery, given the circumstances."

"Oh, Dr. Robinson," she said, "I have complete confidence in you and I know it will work. Please do the surgery."

Believing that her attitude counted for something, and that it might be possible for the procedure to restore some vision, I performed the surgery, in spite of my professional doubts. The procedure couldn't have gone better. Yet, when I examined her one day afterward, she still could not see. She wasn't concerned. She said it was too early to judge the results. "I know I will see, it's just a matter of time," she said.

At her one week visit, nothing had changed. She was using her drops as instructed. I set her up for a one month follow-up. I wanted so much to see her heal and have some useful vision; however, I was beginning to give up hope.

At the last post-op visit one month later, the same dark news—very poor vision, near blindness in the operated left eye. I was very disappointed, but she had not given up hope, even at this point.

Six months later, the same sad encounter. It was very apparent at this visit that everything related to the cataract surgery was perfectly in place and the small wound healed, but still very poor vision. I had to accept that diabetic damage indeed had blinded her remaining eye. Amazingly, she still would not accept my assessment, and once again informed me that someday she would see out of her left eye. I shook my head, wished her well, and said a prayer for her as she left. I said one for me too, that her attitude of unbridled hope would rub off on me. Sad to say, I closed her file; I was sure I had done everything I could to restore her vision.

Two years later, I had all but forgotten this patient, when she scheduled a follow-up appointment with me. I was handed her chart, before I entered the exam room and I couldn't believe my eyes. My technician had recorded the vision in her left eye at 20/25, nearly perfect vision. Was it a patient with the same name? Wrong chart? Could it be? I opened the door and she said as I walked in, "so that's what you look like Dr. Robinson!" Seemingly dwarfed by the exam chair, and with only one leg, I saw a lady with a very big smile on her face.

I can explain things from a medical perspective—she got her diabetes under control with the help of a caring physician. Her cystoid macular edema and diabetic macular edema had cleared, due to good blood sugar control, and miraculously, her rods and cones had realigned almost perfectly. But I know in my heart that it was her hopeful attitude and never giving up hope that allowed healing to occur.

Physicians sometimes are so concerned with facts and science that we need patients to remind us who the Great Physician is.

DR. RANDY ROBINSON

Ophthalmologist
Oklahoma City, OK

WE SHOULD MAKE PLANS—COUNTING ON GOD TO DIRECT US.

PROVERBS 16:9

In my senior year of high school, two days after Christmas, my dad had a massive heart attack and died, leaving my mom with four teenagers, ages 13 to 19. I was angry. We had a huge void in our life. I recall driving by myself at night to the Oral Roberts University parking lot, praying my heart out and expressing anger at God for taking my father when he was only 48 and I was only 17. At the end of my tirade, I asked God to be my father on Earth as well as my father in heaven, and my life has never been the same.

In spite of the grief our family sustained and the financial challenges we faced, God, my Father, blessed our days and provided for our needs in the most amazing ways.

In 1973, during the second semester of my freshman year in college, I was attending Chaminade College in Honolulu, Hawaii. An international cast of the humanitarian singing group *Up With People*, performed on campus. After the performance, a cast member named Joel, from Bartlesville, Oklahoma, encouraged students in the audience to audition/interview for an opportunity to travel, sing, and dance with them the next year. I had always loved to sing and dance and had not seen anyone from Oklahoma in months, so I went down front to talk to him. When he encouraged me to audition, I did. To my amazement, I was accepted. However, when I discovered it cost $3,500 to travel with them, I knew I couldn't go. I had also already committed to being a soloist on a U.S. tour during the next summer with a Congregational Church choir in Hawaii. So I called Joel, explained my financial situation, and declined.

140

But God had other plans. I received a phone call from *Up With People* saying a man named John Rogers from Tulsa had given a $2,500 scholarship for a girl from Tulsa to travel during the next year. Because I was the only girl who had been accepted from Tulsa, *Up With People* said the scholarship was mine. All I had to do was come up with the other $1,000 and figure out the choir dilemma.

I prayed to God and asked him what I should do. I hated to break my commitment to the choir, but I really wanted to travel with *Up With People* too!

As I was praying, I got a phone call from Joel. He told me *Up With People* had to change its starting date at the last minute. Now, it would begin on July 2nd in Newport Beach, California. I had to smile. The choir tour was ending on that same date, in the same town, Newport Beach! Not only that, but the choir tour would pass through Tulsa, so my way home was paid, and I could leave the Hawaii suitcase in Tulsa and take my *Up With People* suitcase to California. God had put all the pieces in place for me! I had to go! Traveling around the world, living with different types of families, and singing songs of peace, love, and hope profoundly impacted my life and cemented my belief that all persons are created equal, are more similar than different, and should be treated with respect. God knew that experience would change my life.

I believe we are supposed to make our plans, but then pray and count on the Holy Spirit to guide us.

HANNAH ROBSON

Community Relations, Williams Companies and Community Volunteer
Tulsa, OK

BUT THEY WHO WAIT FOR THE LORD SHALL RENEW THEIR STRENGTH;
THEY SHALL MOUNT UP WITH WINGS LIKE EAGLES;
THEY SHALL RUN AND NOT BE WEARY;
THEY SHALL WALK AND NOT FAINT.

ISAIAH 40:31

Growing up, faith didn't have to be "taught" in our household, it was practiced as part of our daily life. It was who we were. As far back as I can remember we have always worshipped together, rejoiced together, and prayed together. My parents walked in such strong faith and, as a result, so do my sister and I. For me, faith is like breathing. I cannot live without it.

From a very young age my parents instilled in us the power of patience, persistence, and prayer. They ensured us, as young black women in a relatively young state situated in the southern half of the United States, that the world would indeed catch up. They taught us about our self-worth and the contributions we were responsible for making. They taught us by "walking the walk."

My parents, against all odds, earned their education, made a living for themselves as educators, and raised their family during the height of the civil rights movement. They earned advanced degrees, while working and parenting full time, from the University of Oklahoma when Norman was still considered a "Sundown Town"—an all-white town where people of color were expected to exit the town by sundown.

Always active in school leadership and activities, during high school I was selected for the American Legion Auxiliary's Girls State. At the state convention, I was elected governor by my peers. I was the one chosen to represent Oklahoma at the national convention. However, while still at the state convention, I learned I would be prohibited from serving at the national convention because of my race. I was completely deflated, my self-worth stolen from me. I called my daddy to come pick me up and was waiting with my suitcase at the door when he arrived.

He came to the door, stepped inside, and asked me where I thought I was going. I reminded him that I wasn't able to participate in the national convention. "These girls chose you as their governor, and whether or not you go to the national convention you are still their governor. You stay here and govern and I will pick you up tomorrow when this is over." He left me there in tears, suitcase in hand. I didn't know it then, but Daddy taught me a valuable lesson that night—stand strong in your convictions and He will stand with you.

It was this early experience with racism that shaped my career and led to my commitment to fight for equality for *all*—both here at home and abroad. I reflect on my career and my personal life, my accomplishments and my failures, and know that without the patience, persistence, and the power of prayer instilled in me by my parents I would not and could not be where I am today.

When the world said otherwise, Momma and Daddy knew it would catch up. They knew there was a need for my sister and I and that we would make it as long as we were armed with and stayed true to our faith.

VICKI MILES-LAGRANGE

Judge, United States District Court for the Western District of Oklahoma
and Oklahoma Hall of Fame Inductee
Oklahoma City, OK

TRUST IN THE LORD WITH ALL YOUR HEART.

PROVERBS 3:5

My wife, Lee Anne, and I were sitting in the front row of St. Luke's United Methodist Church in Oklahoma City, the same place we had been married almost four years before, to the day. Only—this day was the memorial service of our eleven-month-old second son, Isaiah Lee. He died when he was 333 days old. Three days earlier, we had awakened to find our precious son dead.

We'd prayed a lot in the previous days, weeks, and months. *Dear God. I think something is wrong with Isaiah. Will you fix it? Amen.*

Then, out loud, *Dear Heavenly Father, we thank Thee for our food. Help us to be grateful, help us to be good. And dear Lord, please help Isaiah get better soon. Amen.*

"Is there anything we can do for you?" countless friends asked.

"Pray for us and especially Isaiah," we said.

I filled out prayer cards for the first time in my life, "Please pray for Isaiah. He keeps having seizures and we cannot figure out what is wrong with him. He is not sleeping at night and it is causing us to be up between five and fifteen times a night. Please pray for patience for both Lee Anne and me because when we are tired and anxious, we yell at each other and it is so uncharacteristic of us. Most importantly, we ask for you to please pray for a diagnosis for Isaiah. Thank you. Renzi and Lee Anne Stone."

And so our prayers at church progressed from week to week.

We prayed with Isaiah's older brother, almost three-year-old Jackson.

144

"Amen" was one of his first words. "Now I lay me down to sleep, I pray the Lord my soul to keep. If I die before I wake, I pray the Lord my soul to take. God bless Mommy, Daddy, Isaiah, Annabelle—our King Charles spaniel— and all my aunts and uncles and grandparents. Make Jackson be a goooood boy! Amen." Sometimes he made a final petition to our God, "please help Isaiah get better."

We believe Jackson knew God's plan for Isaiah before it had been revealed to us.

Finally, Lee Anne and I prayed with each other—the most intense and vulnerable kind of prayer.

Silently I prayed all the time—at meals, in the car, at night, in the morning, between meetings, at the grocery store, and even in the shower.

"Dear God—Please help Isaiah. Help him stop having these seizures. The doctor says that they cannot hurt him, but we hate that he has them and it is terrifying to us. What if we aren't there when one happens? And please help our family have some normalcy. We just want to go a week without a trip to the emergency room or a week with him being completely content. His cries must mean something is wrong, Lord. We are on months of little sleep. More than anything, Lord, please go into Isaiah's head and take out the part of his brain where there is epilepsy. We are your servants, God. Please, we beg of you. Amen."

Looking back at my prayer, I suppose it was answered. I had just never contemplated that our fervent pleas would result in the ultimate healing of death. I had never prayed for him to stay alive. I'd thought God understood that life was implied.

Our time with Isaiah was by far the best *worst* year of our lives. The reality set in that our family of four had been reduced by 25 percent. I cried in front of every friend, co-worker, and casual acquaintance. We decided, after Isaiah left us, that we would lean on each other, we would remain faithful to God, and we would draw on a supernatural strength to get through. We would not crawl in a hole and hide. We would not push those who loved us away because we did not want to talk about our loss. We would be full of grace and dignity. We were weak in the knees, but strong in our hearts.

"Faith," Senior Pastor Dr. Bob Long said towards the end of Isaiah's memorial service, "is not a set of beliefs. Faith is about trust."

Our family chose not to let this loss define us. We will never forget Isaiah and our love for him, but we will also go forward honoring his memory and trusting God for today.

RENZI STONE

Chairman & CEO, Saxum and University of Oklahoma Regent
Oklahoma City, OK

FEAR NOT, FOR I AM WITH YOU; BE NOT DISMAYED, FOR I AM YOUR GOD;
I WILL STRENGTHEN YOU, I WILL HELP YOU, I WILL UPHOLD YOU WITH MY
RIGHTEOUS RIGHT HAND.

ISAIAH 41:10

"Be careful what you wish for" is a saying that we hear very often. A few months before my hospitalization I prayed for a humbling experience… and God gave me one.

I had just finished my first semester at the University of Oklahoma and was home for Christmas break. I was working part-time and trying to enjoy the holidays. I had been having breathing issues for months and had been diagnosed with bronchitis. But then something changed. I started feeling very weak, was irritable, and it became hard to move. It felt like I was treading water; I could barely function. On December 27, 2010 I woke up and could not breathe at all. My mother took me to the emergency room. We assumed they would treat me and send me home. That was not the case.

The last thing I remember is all of the nurses rushing into the room. Eventually diagnosed with severe pneumonia, they intubated me and placed me on a ventilator. I was put into a medically induced coma. The doctors told my parents that I would not make it through the night. However, I kept hearing voices around me saying "Sydney, breathe." I didn't know what they meant, but I just followed their guidance—deep breaths, in and out. The most distinct voice belonged to my mother, telling me over and over again "Sydney, you're in the hospital, you have a tube down your throat to help you breathe." If it had not been for my family encouraging me, I probably would have given up.

During my hospital stay I contracted the H1N1 virus. I could no longer move. I could not use my arms or turn my head. I was completely paralyzed.

With my mouth taped because of the ventilator, I had no way to communicate. I could not ask what was going on, I could not advocate for myself, and I could not tell my family that I could hear them. They just had to sit there and wonder if I would ever be able to understand or communicate again. I was trapped, literally, in my own body.

The moment I will never forget is when I opened my eyes and my mom said "Sydney, blink if you can understand me." You know those movies where someone is stranded on a deserted island and they see a plane or a boat and do everything they can to wave and get attention? That is what it felt like. This was my moment. I blinked as hard as I could, but she wasn't convinced. She said "Blink twice if you can understand me." I blinked twice! She got very excited and called the nurses. A neurologist was called in and an MRI revealed damage to my brain and spinal cord. I was then diagnosed with a rare neurological condition called Acute Disseminated Encephalomyelitis (ADEM). It affected my cervical spinal cord and caused damage to my brainstem.

A tracheostomy was next. I was *thrilled* because it meant that I could get the tube out of my mouth! I remember the first time I was able to mouth real words to my parents. I was finally able to communicate!

The reality of my situation did not actually strike me until I was sent to rehab. I had been lying in bed for almost two months. I had no strength. I could only turn my head, mouth words, and barely move my right hand. Physical therapy consisted of teaching me to sit, because I could no longer sit on my own. It was like a never-ending trust fall. I would sit and cry. I was so scared.

I went home in a wheelchair. I could use my right hand well enough to feed myself. However, that was not enough for me. With multiple rounds of inpatient and outpatient therapy, nothing seemed to help me return to any semblance of normalcy. For every one step forward, it seemed like there were two or more steps backward. Anxiety and depression set in.

It seemed like all of my friends were moving on without me. I felt helpless. I spent my time watching television, listening to music, and feeling down. I started feeling like maybe God was punishing me. I felt like maybe perhaps I didn't deserve to be well or happy. Despite my depression, one thing that lifted me up was the daily support that I received from family and friends on my prayer page.

My life changed when I got a new personal care assistant who modified my room, allowing me to be more independent. She helped me change my mindset. I learned that big changes don't happen overnight and that I needed to do everything I could to get stronger. She also encouraged me to move back to campus.

Jump ahead to the fall of 2018. A recent graduate with a Bachelor's degree in Speech-Language Pathology from the University of Central Oklahoma, I am now a graduate student at Oklahoma State University in Stillwater studying Communication Sciences and Disorders. And yes, I am still living on campus.

I still have many challenges, but I keep holding on to the day when God will help me become less dependent on my wheelchair. As physically and emotionally challenging as this experience has been and will continue to be, I have learned what is important in life. I believe that God gave me this experience to realize how important communication is. It is now my passion to help others communicate. The moral of my story is that God can bring good things out of any situation.

SYDNEY RICH

Oklahoma State University Speech Pathology Major
Oklahoma City, OK

DISCERNMENT IS A SPIRITUAL UNDERSTANDING AND AN EXPERIENTIAL KNOWLEDGE OF HOW GOD IS ACTIVE IN DAILY LIFE THAT IS ACQUIRED THROUGH DISCIPLINED SPIRITUAL PRACTICE. DISCERNMENT IS FAITHFUL LIVING AND LISTENING TO GOD'S LOVE AND DIRECTION SO THAT WE CAN FULFILL OUR INDIVIDUAL CALLING AND SHARED MISSION.

HENRI NOUWEN
Discernment

THE JOY OF THE LORD IS YOUR STRENGTH.

NEHEMIAH 8:10

Wayman and I met at Friendship Church where his dad was pastor. We were both juniors in different high schools in Tulsa. I didn't know he was a big basketball star, being recruited by college coaches from all over America. I just knew that he loved music and had the greatest smile in the world.

Wayman idolized his dad, who taught him that the Lord provides solutions to problems and joy for the journey. Loving God and loving people—*all* people—was Dr. L. L. Tisdale's calling. That was Wayman's life as well. He was the most loving and positive person I've ever known.

Wayman went on to play basketball like few ever have, at Tulsa's Booker T. Washington High School, at the University of Oklahoma, then in the NBA. He set all kinds of records. University of Oklahoma Coach Billy Tubbs changed the team's practice schedule on Sunday so that Wayman could continue to play guitar at his father's church. At OU, Wayman was the first player in any sport to have his jersey number retired. Later, he allowed Blake Griffin to wear it; they became great friends.

Wayman and I married in 1987. Our family was blessed with four incredible children. Wayman would not abide lasting conflict between us or between our children. He would say, "we talked about it, get over it, love each other." And always the smile.

Beyond God and his family, he was dedicated to music and basketball. Music came to him early in his childhood. It was a gift—no lessons—he could hear anything and play it. His successful career as a jazz musician after the NBA was thrilling for him and a big factor in helping him get through his cancer treatment, which was brutal.

In 2007, Wayman fell down some stairs and broke his leg. It was kind of a freak accident. After many tests, the news returned: a malignant tumor in his

151

leg. It was the worst feeling; we fell back on our faith to get us through. There were so many setbacks—the failed initial chemo treatment, another eight weeks of chemo so strong that it put him in bed in a fetal position for weeks, an eight-hour surgery to try and save his leg, then the amputation. After his leg was removed, Wayman welcomed us into his hospital room with a big smile. I thought, well, he's cool with this, so I'm cool. Our youngest child went to his bed and Wayman pulled off the covers for her to see and he promised her that he would be fine. "It's still me," he said. Later he would tell people, "It got my leg, but it didn't get my spirit."

Wayman was everybody's best friend, but especially mine. When he died unexpectedly, I was devastated. We had been told the cancer was gone. We were done with chemo; we were done with all of it. His death was sudden and the result of damage from the radiation treatments. I was blasted into an extended period of disbelief and disconnection. At first I was mad at God because it was so unfair after all Wayman had been through. But in time I've come to just be grateful for his 44 years of accomplishments and my 28 years married to him.

During some of his music shows, Wayman said he would feel an anointing from God and afterwards would learn of how his music had impacted someone that night in a powerful way. Wayman said that music "preached" to him.

His legacy includes a foundation that helps others have mobility through a prosthetic, but his further legacy is the love of God expressed in the way he lived every day and in the way he managed the last years of his life.

These lyrics in a song by Wayman express his faith during that time:

"At night please don't you worry, about the things you goin' through, sometimes they're there for a purpose to show you, He can bring you through."

REGINA TISDALE
Wife of WAYMAN TISDALE

University of Oklahoma and NBA Basketball Player
Tulsa, OK

"FOR I KNOW THE PLANS I HAVE FOR YOU," SAYS THE LORD,
"PLANS TO PROSPER YOU AND NOT TO HARM YOU,
PLANS TO GIVE YOU HOPE AND A FUTURE."

JEREMIAH 29:11

As I gaze back at the landscape of my life, I can hardly believe what God has done. I've been so blessed with three wonderful children, a fine husband of almost 60 years, a meaningful life, friends from the numerous places we lived, and the constant presence of a loving God.

My early years were in Antlers where my mom was divorced and forced to work many jobs—the primary one as a waitress. We lived with her mom, my grandmother, who mostly raised me. I knew we didn't have much, but it never held me back. I managed to excel in high school as a cheerleader, football queen, and even won a few beauty pageants. But, I remember vividly one honor that caused me some pain. I was president of the Future Homemakers of America and the state convention was in Tulsa. The registration cost was $5. We didn't have the money. A teacher offered to pay my way, but instead I chose not to go.

I was 16 years old when I started dating Charlie Stephenson, who was college bound. When I graduated from high school, my mom gave me twenty dollars and found me a ride to Dallas. I packed all my belongings in a little green suitcase and headed south to begin life as a working girl. I got a job with a telephone company for $47 a week. From that salary, I managed to pay my living expenses. Eventually I saved enough to buy a car and even helped my mom.

Charlie and I got engaged the following year and I transferred with the phone company to Oklahoma City and lived at the Y. We were married at the First Presbyterian Church two days after Christmas in 1957. Our two best friends were with us, flowers placed for a wedding later in the day decorated the chapel, and the organist, also there for the large wedding later, played for us as well. The pastor, Raskins Smith, officiated, and had insisted on premarital counseling even for a small wedding. We were blessed by his counsel and friendship.

Charlie graduated with a petroleum engineering degree. He served as an officer in the Army and then became employed in the energy industry. We began a lifetime of professional success and frequent moving …sometimes every six months. The longest we lived anywhere when the kids were growing up was three years in North Dakota.

Our first priority when we transferred to a new town was to find a church. Our faith was important to us as a family and we knew we wanted to get involved in that community. Church helped make that happen and continued to strengthen our bonds as a faith-fueled family.

Charlie's successful career eventually brought us to a permanent home in Tulsa. I've always enjoyed volunteering in my church and my community, but this became even more important when I experienced a health crises. Just a few years ago, I was diagnosed with a fast growing type of breast cancer. A series of mistakes could have created a very different future for me, but instead I had a year of surgeries and treatments and have been cancer free since. From the very beginning, I felt God in my heart. I was never overwhelmed with fear because of His presence. I was anxious for my family, knowing their concern for my wellbeing, but I was totally surrounded by God's love. It was as if a light bulb had been turned on and I could see the world in a different light. So many friends prayed for me, as well as my family, and special Bible Study friends were daily prayer warriors. I know with my whole being that the power of prayer changed my life during that time.

As a result of my gratitude, I work in Tulsa for Project Woman, which helps fund breast cancer screenings and education for women with limited resources. And Charlie and I have helped establish the Stephenson Cancer Center at the University of Oklahoma Heath Sciences Center in Oklahoma City. One of my favorite things to do is drop by that center and strike up a conversation with someone who seems to be in need. Maybe they are a patient or a family member of a patient. God helps me to recognize their pain or their fear and I just visit with them and offer encouragement. I always leave with a blessing and a promise that I will pray for those who are affected by this disease.

I have been blessed in so many ways; to be able to be a vehicle of God's hope to others is the greatest honor. And for this girl from Pushmataha County whose grandfather was a bootlegger, I can say with all sincerity, you never know what plans God has for you but *hope* will always be a part of it.

PEGGY CLARK STEPHENSON

Volunteer, Philanthropist, Co-Founder, Stephenson Family Foundation,
and Oklahoma Hall of Fame Inductee
Antlers/Tulsa, OK

THEREFORE EVERYONE WHO HEARS THESE WORDS OF MINE
AND PUTS THEM INTO PRACTICE IS LIKE A WISE MAN
WHO BUILT HIS HOUSE ON THE ROCK.
THE RAIN CAME DOWN, THE STREAMS ROSE, AND THE WINDS BLEW
AND BEAT AGAINST THAT HOUSE; YET IT DID NOT FALL,
BECAUSE IT HAD ITS FOUNDATION ON THE ROCK.
BUT EVERYONE WHO HEARS THESE WORDS OF MINE AND DOES NOT
PUT THEM INTO PRACTICE IS LIKE A FOOLISH MAN
WHO BUILT HIS HOUSE ON SAND. THE RAIN CAME DOWN,
THE STREAMS ROSE, AND THE WINDS BLEW AND BEAT AGAINST
THAT HOUSE, AND IT FELL WITH A GREAT CRASH.

MATTHEW 7:24-27

Here's something I have to admit—I am no fan of televangelists. I tire of hearing people in the public eye go on and on about their religion. However, I discovered that as I put together my recent book, *Turpen Time*, many of the chapters had spiritual stories from my life.

Hypocritical? Maybe. I believe deeply that people should live their faith instead of just *talking* about it. Turn your theology into your biography. As I wrote about my faith in my stories, it was always in conjunction with how that belief was *lived*.

This brings me to the case of Sally Ross and to one of my favorite passages of scripture, Matthew 7:24-27—building our house on the rock.

Sally Ross was a devout Christian. She built her house on rock, not sand. Sally was not only able to withstand a relentless and well-financed courtroom attack on her personal character, but she was able to reach even greater heights as a dedicated, committed public servant. In the early 1980's Sally served as Tahlequah's city clerk. However, in 1988 the city sued her for $21,000, alleging that in 1981 she had placed her disabled husband on the city's insurance policy without approval from the City Council. She was charged with embezzlement. It was a bad case and a cheap shot. The powers-that-be were concerned she was planning to run for mayor.

Sally supported me during my run for Oklahoma Attorney General. She remained a loyal friend after my unsuccessful run for governor in 1986. She rode the river with me, and now as an attorney in private practice, I was there for her. People were flown in from all over, testifying that she didn't have permission to deduct the insurance premium.

I don't have a transcript of my closing argument, but I do remember saying: "Ladies and gentlemen: Everybody's against Sally Ross—everybody but the people. The powerful don't want Sally to run for mayor, because they can't control her. She is her own person. What you see is what you get with Sally Ross." To be honest, I was in trouble with the case. There had been a lot of collaboration to ensure all of the stories against Sally painted a bleak picture for her. It wasn't a criminal proceeding; I wasn't trying to save her freedom. However, I was trying to save her honorable reputation. They wanted to take away her livelihood and, with it, any political future she might have in Cherokee County.

That night I could not fall asleep. After praying to God for His divine intervention, I felt a certain peace. I knew that the decision was not only in the hands of the jury, but in a far higher power. I could do nothing more.

The jury came back with a *not guilty* verdict. Sally and I hugged. I shared with her my doubts about the outcome. She then handed me a crumpled piece of green construction paper with the following words inscribed:

When all has been done that can be done,
Though this, to some, may seem very odd,
The paramount need appears to be
Just letting go and letting God.

It's like closing the door, wrapping oneself
In a kind of solitary pod,
And there in faith-filled quietness
Just letting go and letting God.

No need to struggle or plead the prayer,
For when mind and heart no longer plod,
Amazingly, the answer comes—
Just letting go and letting God.

I jokingly told her, "Sally, why didn't you tell me sooner? I would not have spent so much time on my knees at the motel?" In the end, though, I knew that the peace I'd felt after I'd finished my petition to the Almighty was like the peace that the poem brought to her throughout the trial. Both of us had to let go and let God!

And, by the way, Sally Ross served as the first female mayor of Tahlequah from 1989 to 1995.

MIKE TURPEN

Attorney, Author, Television Host, and Former Attorney General
Tulsa/Muskogee/Oklahoma City, OK

FOR NOTHING WILL BE IMPOSSIBLE WITH GOD.

LUKE 1:37

What does he look like, this Jesus? Is he really European with beautiful, light brown hair? Even when you really think about it, imagining what Jesus might look like is difficult, but like everyone else, I think I might know.

I suppose that each person has their own opinion and can picture him, just so.

Quite often, that image is based on European art over the ages; portrayals of Christ as such a lovely man, graceful and slim. He might even look like that young man down the block or he might look like our oldest son, who is even the right age. Art beguiles us though when we try to envision him.

From the earliest days, Jesus has been portrayed in a particular way, I'm not sure why.

Jesus was a Jew. Two thousand years ago. He would have looked like other Jewish men. He would have been dark of skin and hair, strong of features.

I believe that if he had stood out as this beautiful, blond creature, there would have been no problem in the people proclaiming him King and following him, in mass, to whack the Romans. It would have been easy.

But don't you see, it ain't easy. It isn't supposed to be. Easy has no virtue. Jesus had to look like all the other men. The Disciples and all the others followed Him, not because of the way he looked, but because of the fire within Him, the Grace and power of His words, the overwhelming assurance of his promise.

Jesus had to be like the other men. He sweated and smelled like the others. He slept when he tired, and ate when he was hungry. However, He shared His relationship with God with the others only as they were able to understand. Those men, as with us today, would have been unwilling to accept our limitations to that perfect understanding. That's why we must have Faith. Faith, alone, overcomes all understanding.

I have looked at Jesus in my dreams and to me, His image is like that on the Shroud of Turin. I choose to believe that is His image on that cloth. Many swear that it is not. Swearing is not good, you know. Whether it is, or not, there is no way to know. It has no effect on me personally. I look at the Shroud as a gift.

I, like everyone else, will ultimately see what He looks like when we see Him in Heaven. But, there is one person who I believe might know, even now, what Jesus looks like, his name is Joey.

Joey is blind.

Joey is blind and has been since his birth. Joey was also born with Down Syndrome. He is a treasure, an Angel.

Joey and his father have been going to St. Francis Xavier much longer than Martha and I. In fact, as a man in his 50's, he's been going there all of his life. He makes his presence known. He is quite loud and often speaks out of turn. Interesting though, he knows most of the songs by heart and sometimes speaks the Liturgy along with the Priest. Sometimes he will grow obviously tired during the Homily and sigh and speak up grandly, "Well Jesus Christ."

Our Priest will have to bow his head, not in prayer but in an effort to control his laughter.

Joey is a delight and I always try and touch his shoulder when I pass by he and his father on my way to Communion. I will have touched an Angel. I have always felt that behind those useless eyes and simple countenance is a man of extreme value. If nothing else, I look at him and count my incredible blessings.

I am an artist. My eyes are everything to me. Everything.

I have a cousin; she has a very difficult time speaking. She loves the fact that, in fact, I am an artist. That I am artistic. She will introduce me to someone she knows as, and proudly pronounce me... "this my cousin, he autistic."

Maybe, she's right.

One of my favorite movies is *Little Big Man*. In that movie, a young man helps his grandfather to the old man's burial platform. The old man is blind from a war wound many years before. He dances and sings his death song. He thanks the Great Spirit for his many victories and defeats and for all that he had seen. He thanks him again, for his blindness in which he saw more. He saw further. He saw the impossible.

I wonder about Joey. What does he see? Has he indeed seen things that I cannot? Has he seen Jesus as Jesus can be seen ...only through the eyes of the blind?

MIKE LARSEN

Native American Artist and Oklahoma Hall of Fame Inductee
Wynnewood/Oklahoma City/Perkins, OK

BE JOYFUL ALWAYS; PRAY CONTINUALLY;
GIVE THANKS IN ALL CIRCUMSTANCES,
FOR THIS IS GOD'S WILL FOR YOU IN CHRIST JESUS.

1 THESSALONIANS 5:17

My effort to console a friend, over a loss, turned into spiritual gain for me. I learned that *practice* doesn't make perfect—but it can make the best possible. The discipline of a daily spiritual commitment grows a strong connection to a power source that helps us overcome circumstances.

Meeting Kay Dudley for lunch was my chance to comfort her following the death of her husband of 52 years.

She greeted me with a hug and a smile. No outward sign of grief or health problems—not even a mention of her recent wrestling match with painful shingles.

"God is so good," she said. "I miss Tom, of course, but my life is so blessed."

After many painful brushes with death, Kay's husband's passing had been peaceful. She remembered "We sat in our easy chairs for our daily devotional time—and I glanced over and he was gone.

"The doctors brought his pulse back, and he lingered in ICU for several days—just time for all the children to gather.

"They called us to his room in time for the final breath, and we circled the bed to pray for his journey into God's hands and give thanks for his life. The doctor said he'd never witnessed a family so peaceful and joyful at a death.

"God is so good."

Sitting across from Kay in that restaurant with all the clutter of lunch and life, I felt the sadness of her loss but also the joy of her relationship with the Father.

There was an inner strength that few Christians really live out daily. I'd known this woman for many years and that strong faith and goodness were always present.

How do *we* get there? I took that question to my spiritual director, Sister Benedicta. "If the goal of spiritual growth is deep intimacy with God—a closeness that is known from morning to night, not just in daily prayer—how does that happen," I asked?

Without hesitation, she answered. "Practice."

Sister Benedicta, an 86-year-old blessing, whose wisdom and love have affected so many, could teach on spiritual discipline and other tenets for years, but she offered just one word.

"Practice," she said.

I understand working toward a defined goal in other disciplines: daily shooting exercises in order to win a basketball game; constant singing of musical scales to produce a flexible voice that will be cast in the lead role of a musical; days of preparation and research before standing up to influence others in a speech; and years of putting words on the page before a known publisher is interested in your book.

Practice devotion, reverence, awareness, thanksgiving, service, *practice being with God*? I'm accustomed to working on goals with a deadline but this is an ongoing commitment for life. I kept wondering how I keep motivated with so many other activities vying for my time and attention. "Any other words of advice on exactly how I can do this," I asked?

Sister said to keep asking God for the *desire* to be aware of Him, and that practice would reveal results.

Christians who live with a continual closeness to God have a special peace, a kindness that is consistent, and a deep joy.

Believers, like Kay and Sister B, have practiced for so many years; it is now second nature for them to live in a posture of prayer. Communicating with God isn't something that begins with "Dear" and ends with "Amen" occasionally. It's a way of life that begins with *real* time with God and grows from there. We *practice* being with God so that everything about our lives begins to be filtered through this Holy relationship. And when a crisis comes, as it does for everyone, believers—who have practiced so well and for so long—look at the trouble, the heartache, the fear, the despair and say: *God is so good!*

JANE JAYROE

Former Miss America, News Anchor, Author, and Oklahoma Hall of Fame Inductee
Laverne/Oklahoma City, OK

IF WE FILL OUR SOULS WITH

LOVE

WE'D HAVE NO ROOM FOR HATE;

IF WE FILL OUR HEARTS WITH

PASSION

WE'D HAVE NO ROOM FOR APATHY;

IF WE FILL OUR SPIRITS WITH

FAITH

WE'D HAVE NO ROOM FOR DESPAIR;

AND IF WE'D FILL OUR LIVES WITH

GOD

WE'D HAVE NO ROOM FOR FEAR.

DR. HANNA SAADAH

AFTERWORD

It is the greatest honor to be trusted with the faith stories of others. I pray these devotional pieces have inspired you. God knows, how they grew my faith in working through each and every one of them. My deepest appreciation to each author for his or her contribution.

Also, I'm so grateful to my friend, the talented photographer David Fitzgerald for his beautiful capturing of an Oklahoma sunrise that graces the cover of this book.

Immense gratitude to Gini Moore Campbell and Oklahoma Hall of Fame Publishing for their editing help and friendship. Profits from this project will benefit this organization, which is dedicated to telling Oklahoma's story through its people. Thousands of young Oklahomans find their own dreams through hearing about the lives of our state's heroes.

JANE JAYROE